Books by Mary Washington Clarke

INTRODUCING FOLKLORE
[with Kenneth Clarke as co-author]

A FOLKLORE READER
[with Kenneth Clarke as co-author]

JESSE STUART'S KENTUCKY

JESSE STUART'S KENTUCKY

JESSE
STUART'S
KENTUCKY

by Mary Washington Clarke

McGRAW-HILL BOOK COMPANY
New York   Toronto   London   Sydney

Acknowledgment is made to the following sources for permission to reprint from material already published:

Man with a Bull-Tongue Plow by Jesse Stuart. Copyright © 1934, 1959 by Jesse Stuart. Dutton Paperback Edition. Reprinted by permission of E. P. Dutton & Co., Inc.

The Thread That Runs So True by Jesse Stuart. Copyright © 1949 by Charles Scribner's Sons.

For permission to reprint the list of Awards and Honors, permission granted by David Brandenburg, editor of the *W-Hollow Harvest*, in the announcement of the limited W-Hollow binding of *Taps for Private Tussie.*

For all other quotations from the writings of Jesse Stuart, permission granted by Jesse Stuart and by the McGraw-Hill Book Company.

Library of Congress Catalog Card Number: 68-18575
First Edition   11238

For the people of our Southern Mountains, whose heritage and destiny I share, and for the man who has given them a voice in the literature of our time

Jesse Stuart
Awards and Honors*

1934 Jeanette Sewal Davis Poetry Prize

1937 Guggenheim Fellowship Award for Creative Writing and European Travel

1941 Academy of Arts and Science Award of $500 for *Men of the Mountains*

1943 Thomas Jefferson Memorial Award, $2,500, for *Taps for Private Tussie*

1943 *Taps for Private Tussie*, Book of the Month Club Selection

1944 Honorary Doctor of Literature, University of Kentucky

1946 *Man with a Bull-Tongue Plow* selected as one of the 100 Best Books in America and one of the 1,000 Great Books of the World

1949 *The Thread That Runs So True* selected as the best book in 1949 by the National Education Association

1950 Honorary Doctor of Humanities, Lincoln Memorial University

1952 *Taps for Private Tussie* selected as one of the masterpieces of world literature

1952 Honorary Doctor of Literature, Marietta College

* As prepared by David Brandenburg, editor of *W-Hollow Harvest*, in the announcement of the limited W-Hollow Binding of *Taps for Private Tussie*.

1954 Poet Laureate of Kentucky

1954 Honorary Doctor of Laws, Baylor University

1955 Berea College Centennial Award for Literature

1956 Jesse Stuart Memorial Dedicated, Greenup, Kentucky

1958 Honored on "This Is Your Life" Television program

1959 Honorary Doctor of Literature, Morris Harvey College

1961 The Academy of American Poets Award, $5,000, for "Distinguished Service to American Poetry"

1962 Honorary Doctor of Literature, Marshall University

1964 Honorary Doctor of Literature, Northern Michigan University

1964 Honorary Doctor of Literature, Eastern Kentucky University

1966 Honorary Doctor of Literature, Berea College

1966 Dedication of Jesse Stuart High School, Valley Station, Kentucky

1967 W-Hollow Anniversary Binding of *Taps for Private Tussie,* Commemorating his sixtieth anniversary

1967 *W-Hollow Harvest,* a magazine for Jesse Stuart buffs, began publication

1967 Awarded the Pilgrim Medal, Defiance College, Defiance, Ohio

Author's Preface

I first saw and heard Jesse Stuart in West Virginia in the middle 1930s, not long after the publication of *Man With a Bull-Tongue Plow*. The charm of the familiar in a novel setting appealed to me then and kept me reading Stuart's poems and stories as they appeared in widely diversified publications over the years. I knew his characters, their speech, and their way of life well. Three generations of my family—the Washingtons, Somervilles, Braggs, and Huddlestons—grew up in similar communities in Appalachia. I know the culture as it was and as it is. Most members of my generation are college-educated, and many of us have gone urban, but we still use our old recipes for sulphuring apples, making pickles, and baking bread. We still use many of the old folk sayings. We still have big family reunions. We enjoy our traditions and one another without romanticizing or deploring our rural backgrounds.

I gradually developed an academic interest in the authenticity of Stuart's materials, especially when I could privately enjoy the extra dimension of unintended comedy arising from city-bred critics whose reviews expressed incredulity or denunciations when Stuart was being most accurate. My interests in folklore and regional speech carried me to Stuart's own home region, on both the West Virginia and Kentucky sides of the Big Sandy River, for field collecting. I tape recorded the speech, sayings, songs, and tales of hill people for analysis and annotation. I have been impressed with the number of rare, or relatively rare, beliefs, expressions, and activities that Stuart's retentive memory and ability at mimicry have relayed into his works. Anyone who reads *Trees of Heaven, Taps for Private Tussie,* or a sampling of his short stories with an open mind will understand better why the welfare agencies cannot suddenly and conclusively win an anti-poverty war in Appalachia.

It is my hope that my own distillation of Jesse Stuart's positive view of life, past and present, may have a two-fold influence: that it may clarify some misconceptions of our much discussed and much misunderstood region, and that it may contribute to a growing awareness that an original writer is speaking to the world for us.

The genesis of this book has involved many friends and relatives, to whom I have already expressed my gratitude. I do wish to mention here, however, a few who have gone beyond the demands of friendship. I am indebted to Dr. Gordon Wilson, Sr., emeritus professor of English at Western Kentucky University, for allowing me to use his extensive files of Kentucky folklore and folk speech. He has assisted me with verification of a number of puzzling folk locutions. I am deeply indebted to Miss Frances Richards, emeritus professor of English at Western Kentucky University and long-time specialist on Kentucky literature, who read the entire manuscript with great care and supplied valuable criticism. Helpful comments were also given by Mrs. Doris Miller, a former newspaper colleague of mine on the Huntington (W. Va.) *Herald-Advertiser;* and by Mr. Loyal Jones, Executive Director of the Council of the Southern Mountains.

Contents

JESSE STUART'S KENTUCKY

Introduction

When Jesse Stuart wrote *My Land Has a Voice* he wrote truly, for his land, his Kentucky, does indeed have a voice, and that voice is his. Jesse Stuart of W-Hollow, farmer, poet, novelist, educator, prophet in his own time, speaks the poetry of the dark hills of his birth—his natural voice.

Some other regional writers have attempted the folkways and dialects of their subjects and have failed because theirs has been imitation, the self-conscious and too often patronizing effort to depict what one sees and hears but does not *know*. Stuart expresses the hill man's deep feelings about God, man, and the seasons because these are his own feelings. While the imitator captures some of the surface oddities of dialect, Stuart goes all the way, faithfully presenting the anachronisms, irregularities, and paradoxes of an antique speech caught up in rapid shift toward modernity.

Some romantic nostalgia for sloughed-off traditions accompanies every step forward, with a sigh here and there for the old country-style parties and dances, the spelling and arithmetic bees, the brush-arbor revivals, the Fourth-of-July celebrations, and basket dinners. Stuart knows that even a land happy with its outmoded ways cannot be a Shangri-la. The world moves in, exploiting that very love of tradition, for the older people especially have shied away from riding the wild horse of modern progress and from learning to be shrewd in the modern sense of getting ahead. Such a land in transition is the W-Hollow country which Jesse Stuart has given a voice.

His Kentucky is not all of Kentucky, but, like Robert

Burns' Scotland and William Faulkner's Mississippi, it is
that corner of the earth the author has taken up to be a part
of himself. Stuart wrote "Come Take This Tour with Me,"
an article about his home area. Those who take a tour
through his range of writing will see as surely as in Chaucer's pilgrimage to Canterbury a microcosm of humanity, a
wise and comic metaphor of life.

Geographically, the Stuart country is limited to Greenup,
Carter, and Floyd counties and the bordering areas along
the westernmost edge of the Cumberland Plateau. Tangled,
snake-infested thickets, moss-grown rock cliffs, and a vein-
work of unpredictable creeks and branches isolated Jesse
Stuart's Kentucky for many generations from the busy Ohio
River Valley between Huntington, West Virginia, and
Portsmouth, Ohio.

By a set of freakish circumstances, a sensitive boy, a born
poet, survived all the physical and psychological threats of
his surroundings. With odds almost incalculable against
success in the venture, he went out into the world and
achieved a higher education. And then, contrary to normal
expectations, he chose to return to the land of his birth.
This return from exile (in the ancient pattern of the folk
hero) brought a cutting edge to the tool so improbably
shaped—a veritable bull-tongue plow of literature. Here is
a native son in the truest sense, but a native son with an extra dimension—an objectivity that permits him to see truly
and depict faithfully the love and hate, the comedy and
tragedy, the beauty and bestiality of a unique passing
pocket of American culture.

And how desirable this is! For no other region has been
the subject of so much misunderstanding and misinterpre-
tation by curious outsiders and sensation seekers in recent
decades. The very word *folklore* has a certain magic—so
much so that it has been shamefully exploited and abused
by those who "know the price of everything and the value

of nothing." In this exploitation, eastern Kentucky has become almost synonymous with the word. But *folklore* for the opportunistic exploiter usually implies sensational foolishness, crudities of all kinds, and practices that have no apparent purpose other than to produce a guffaw on cue. Stuart knows folklore, not for the label, but for what it is—the traditions that make up a part of a way of life. It is significant that professor-scholar Gordon Wilson, Kentucky's senior folklorist, was the first editor to accept for publication a piece of writing by Jesse Stuart, and to advise the young writer to stay in Kentucky. From that first acquaintance in 1928 grew a friendship and mutual respect that persist after almost forty years to the time of this writing.

The extremes of fundamentalism and luxuriant proliferation of the subdivisions of the Mountain Baptist Church have become the subject of amused comment, even among the members of the various sects. Stuart's relative objectivity derived from education and cosmopolitan experience makes him unique among the participant-observers of the hill man's religion. He has not singled out religion for separate treatment. It is, rather, woven through his decades of writing as the closely integrated aspect of mountaineer life he knows it to be.

A hill man's pleasure is also inextricably involved with his folklore and religion. Indeed, the hill man has had a peculiar talent for finding pleasure even in his work—if he worked at the soil-bound tasks of tradition instead of the dehumanizing labor of industry.

Jesse Stuart knows a hill man's work, for his earliest memories are tied to the cultivation of the land. No stranger, he, to the double-bitted ax, the singletree, and the bull-tongue plow. Now, as a successful author and landowner, he gives more attention to conserving and restoring the exploited land than to wresting a living from it. But the love of the soil and the restorative power of nature are in him—and in all he writes.

The hill man's schools, both as they were when Jesse the boy carried his lunch pail and as they are—so far progressed in (and partly because of) one man's lifetime— figure in one of America's best-loved books about schools: *The Thread That Runs So True.* Stuart is dedicated in many ways to many things, but his dedication to education and his consequent contribution loom large in his career.

Finally, there is the land with its changing faces of beauty through the cycles of the seasons, scarred and defaced here and there by the careless hand of man, but able to restore itself if permitted to do so. And in that act of restoration the land gives an article of faith to those who take their living from it by the sweat of their brow in a primitive setting. Is it this certainty that Nature will provide if man will perform his share of the labor that produces the rugged independence of mind and spirit so characteristic of the hill man?

Folklore, religion, pleasures, schools, work, and setting: these are the aspects of Stuart's works presented in the following chapters. This sampling is a distillation from his many novels, articles, and short stories. It is intended to reveal Stuart the insider, the man who knows. Like Chaucer and Mark Twain and ever so many other great writers before him, he revels in the language and lore of the whole spectrum of humanity as he sees it. He writes of the crudities and cruelties along with the bounties and beauties of his land. And, most important, when he injects the spirit of comedy, he does so with acceptance and compassion, for he is not one of the "angry young men." When he laughs, he laughs *with* his people, not at them. When he chides for wrongheadedness and self-destructive conservatism, he chides as an understanding neighbor or brother, not as an intruding reformer.

CHAPTER ONE

The Folklore of a Kentucky Hill Community

A land that has kept its traditions. . . .

KENTUCKY IS MY LAND

Jesse Stuart's writings contain a rich sampling of the diversified folklore of his Kentucky hill community—doleful ballads of death and false true-loves, rollicking country dance calls, ghostly visitations and a superstition for every occasion, weather and planting lore, a *yarb* for every ill that man has fallen heir to, tall tales of men and animals, and humor both broad and grim.

Some Stuart characters, like their real-life counterparts, are veritable repositories of folklore. A favorite of Stuart's in his writings and in real life has been Uncle Op Akers, the central character of *The Good Spirit of Laurel Ridge*, yarb doctor and tale-teller par excellence. Notable for his store of local legends as well as other types of lore has been Uncle Uglybird, gravedigger and water witch. Granny Flaugherty, who lived almost to the century mark before she *went to be one of God's angels*, figures prominently in the folklore of death and the afterlife. Old Peter Leadingham's exploits have provided a whole cycle of hill preacher stories. Uncle

5

Mel Shelton, Uncle Rank Larks, and all the other old dads, grandpas, and grandmas of Stuart's fiction have developed from real people—people closely identified with the old folk culture. Stuart's genial tolerance of their superstitions and his delight in the old songs and tales show how deeply he himself has drunk of Kentucky's *lonesome waters*.

Certain original elements in Stuart's stories and some parts of his autobiographical writings that purport to be factual seem to have sprung from the same impulses that preserve folklore in oral tradition: the workings of the folk mind with its sense of identification with nature, its delight in the fantastic and wonderful, its taste for grotesque exaggerations and clever trickery. Some items are very similar to those collected in other parts of the highlands; some are strongly localized. The de-emphasis on motivation and the focus on situation, the use of folk clichés and grotesque similes that bother little about verisimilitude, frequent use of the present tense, and a ballad-like repetition have also contributed to the authentic folk flavor of Stuart's work.

Although the Stuarts were not a singing family, an incident from one of Jesse Stuart's college vacations showed his taste for the sad old *lonesome songs*. His mother was *kindly mad* that he had not come directly home: "Mom, I heard 'Loving Nancy' played and sung the sweetest I've ever heard it. A blind man and his blind wife played 'Loving Nancy' and a lot of other ballads I've heard all my life. I just couldn't get out of Greenup." In the blind couple's repertory were also "The Hangman's Song," "Pretty Polly," and "The Little Mohee."

In keeping with the changing times, Stuart's allusions to mountain music have included sentimental love songs and hillbilly songs along with the older traditional songs and ballads. Symanthia Fiddler's cross-eyed Greenup beau sang "Those Brown Eyes." The old-time musicians in Greenup sometimes sang "Frankie and Johnnie." "Careless Love" and

"Darlin' Cora" were favorites of the Tussie boys. The two-stepping Muff Henderson sang as he danced his perpetual shuffle down a Blakesburg street, "Around my neck's a golden chain, and every link in Jesus name," lines from the spiritual "Keep Your Hand on the Plow."

Scattered through Stuart's writings are references to songs, and brief passages from them; but, with the exception of occasional religious songs and traditional ballads in his first autobiography, *Beyond Dark Hills,* he gives few full song texts. "Red Wing," "Red River Valley," "Down by the Old Mill Stream," "Listen to the Mockingbird," and "Little Rosewood Casket" were popular in the same neighborhoods where "Barbara Allan" was a favorite. Less common, but current, were the crude homemade ballads such as Jud Sparks' tribute to a local boy. Most of them were in a more serious vein, dealing with mine accidents, war deaths, and other disasters, and would have evoked tears rather than the laughing and clapping that rewarded Sparkie for his song of the boy who "whittled on the telephone post where men had whittled before," and was put "in the jailhouse where he had been just twice before."

Improvisations and adaptations of sentimental songs such as Uncle George Tussie's "Carry Me Back to the Mountains" and Hoot Hammertight's "The Hoot Owl Song" were typical of the time and place. Hoot sings the latter to guitar accompaniment:

> Oh, when you hear that hoot owl callin'
> It's gonna turn cold, it's gonna turn cold;
> And when you see my teardrops fallin',
> I'm thinkin' of the days of old.
>
> I don't know why I love you, darlin',
> It's plain you never cared for me;
> But still my mind is on you, darlin',
> It makes no difference where I be.

I'm goin' down to the deep blue river,
Down where the cool sweet waters flow;
Gonna lay me down and sleep forever,
Down where the snow-white lilies blow.

Oh, bury me beside the river
Where the nightingales sing sweet and low,
There let me rest in peace forever,
Down where the cool sweet waters flow.

Where the fog is on the deep blue river
And the mist is on the mountain high
And the nightingale sings in the twilight,
There let me slumber when I die. . . .

When you hear that hoot owl callin',
It's time to plant corn, it's time to plant corn;
And when you wake and hear sweet music,
It's the nightingale at the break of morn.

And the singer wiped from his eye a tear, which would seem to have had more justification if it followed Stuart's text of "Pretty Polly." Songs of prisoners, neglected sweethearts, and unrequited love—often in a very sentimental vein—were as popular among the hill folk as the songs of murder and fatal accidents.

Hootbird also sang "The Little Rosewood Casket" and the somewhat lighter "Goin' Back to Lickin' ":

Woke up this mornin'
Before the break of day,
Thought about my darlin'
A thousand miles away. . . .

Some says I won't
And some say I will
Go back to Lickin'
To get my bottle filled. . . .

> Standin' in the depot,
> And I seen a train go by;
> I thought about my darlin'
> And hung my head and cried. . . .
>
> I'm goin' back to Lickin',
> I'm goin' back today;
> I'm goin' back to Lickin'
> And there I'm goin' to stay.

Old Op remarked that he had not heard the song for forty years.

Stuart placed "Down in the Valley," known throughout his hills and almost universally throughout the United States, in the context of a molasses-making. The people sang it as they approached and as they left:

> Down in the valley, valley so low,
> Hang your head over, hear the wind blow;
> Hear the wind blow, Love, hear the wind-blow;
> Hang your head over, hear the wind blow.
>
> Down in the valley, down on my knees,
> Praying to Heaven to give my heart ease;
> Give my heart ease, Love, give my heart ease,
> Praying to Heaven to give my heart ease.
>
> Down in the meadow, the mockingbird sings,
> Telling my story, here's what she sings:
> Roses love sunshine, violets love dew,
> Angels in Heaven know I love you.
>
> Write me a letter, send it by mail,
> Send it in care of Greenupsburg jail;
> Greenupsburg jail, Love, Greenupsburg jail,
> Send it in care of the Greenupsburg jail.

And the closing stanza repeated the first one.

Stuart's song texts have shown local adaptation in certain details, as in "Down in the Valley," but are interesting chiefly as an indication of the transitional state of folk music in his locality in the middle decades of the twentieth century before the hootenanny era further blurred distinctions. "On Top of Old Smoky," which exists in many texts throughout the hills, contains the *railroad* detail in Stuart's text:

> She'll hug you and kiss you
> And tell you more lies,
> Than crossties in the railroad
> Or the stars in the skies.

"The Hangman's Song" reverses the sexes of "The Maid Freed from the Gallows," a natural change in a community where men but not women had been executed at public hangings. The text, almost identical with the one Evelyn Wells recorded in Harlan County, Kentucky, in 1916, inserts the following floating lines in the first two stanzas after Pa and Ma refuse to pay the man's fine:

> Oh won't you love and it's hard to be beloved
> And it's hard to make up your time,
> You have broke the hearts of many a love, true love,
> True love, but you won't break mine.

It then closes with the stanza:

> "Hangman, Hangman, slack up your rope,
> O slack it for a while,
> I looked over yonder and I see my sweetheart comin',
> She's walked for many a long mile."

> "Sweetheart, Sweetheart, have you brung me any gold,
> Any gold for to pay my fine?"
> "Yes sir, yes, sir, I've brought you some gold,

Some gold for to pay your fine,
For I've just come for to take you home,
From on the gallows line."

Stuart's text of "The Little Mohee" contains the "coconut grove" setting, popular in southern West Virginia and northeastern Kentucky and collected in many other places where there are no coconut groves; the text follows the basic story. His "Pretty Polly" tells a familiar and ever-popular ballad story of a girl courted, murdered, and buried by her false lover:

In London far city a lady did dwell,
Concerning her beauty no tongue can tell.

He courted Pretty Polly the livelong night,
And then just to rob her before daylight.

"Come home, Pretty Polly, and go along with me,
Before we get married some pleasure we'll see."

He led her over hills and through valleys so deep,
At last Pretty Polly began for to weep.

"Willie, oh, Willie, I'm afraid of your ways,
I'm afeared you're a-leadin' my body astray."

She trusted him a piece farther and what did she spy,
But a new-dug grave and two spades a-lying by.

"Polly, Pretty Polly, you're guessing just right,
I've finished your grave I was digging last night."

She threw her arms around him, she trembled with fear,
"How can you kill a poor girl that loves you so dear?"

"No time for to talk, no time for to stand,"
He came with his knife all in his right hand.

He stabbed her to the heart and the heart blood did flow,
Down in her grave Pretty Polly must go.

He threw the sod over her and he turned to go home,
And left little birds to weep and to mourn.

The word choice shows localization, but the reference to
"the little birds to weep and to mourn" suggests old ballads.
No vestige remains of the resourceful lady of "Lady Isabel
and the Elf-Knight," who cleverly turned the tables.

"Loving Nancy" combines the "Cuckoo Song" with "The
Wagoner's Lad" stanzas:

> The heart is the fortune of all womenkind,
> They are always controlled, but are always confined;
> Controlled by their parents until they are wives,
> Then slaves for their husbands the rest of their lives.

> I've always been a poor girl, my fortune has been bad,
> I've often been courted by the wagoner's lad;
> He courted me daily by night and by day,
> And then for to leave me and going away.

> My parents don't like me because I am poor,
> They say I'm not worthy of entering their door;
> I work for my living, my money's my own,
> And if they don't like me they can leave me alone.

> The cuckoo is a pretty bird, she sings as she flies,
> She gives us glad tidings, she tells us no lies;
> She feeds on sweet flowers to make her voice clear
> And never hollas "cuckoo" 'till spring of the year.

> "Go put up your horses and feed them some hay,
> Come sit you down by me, while you have to stay."
> "My horses are not hungry, they won't eat your hay,
> So farewell, Loving Nancy, I'll feed on the way."

> "Your wagon needs greasing, your bill is to pay,
> Come and sit you down by me, while you have to stay."
> "My wagon is greasy, my whip's in my hand,
> So farewell, Loving Nancy, I've no time for to stand."

Stuart's singers and their instruments, as much as the songs themselves, showed the transition at work in mountain music. Weak-witted Hootbird Hammertight, who was "a-takin' lessons on the geetar," showed the influence of the easy lessons by correspondence on hill music. Uncle George Tussie, who could "make a fiddle cry and laugh" and "could almost make it talk," knew every tune anyone could request and improvised like an ancient bard; the fiddle even now is the true folk instrument, closest of all to the hearts of hill musicians. The tobacco-chewing, fox-hunting, pistol-packing teenager Jud Sparks sang his homemade ballad without accompaniment. Uncle Mott Tussie twanged sad songs on his *banjer*, but could never equal the magic of Uncle George's fiddle. Nancy Cochrane and Flossie Conway sang to guitar accompaniment to while away the time in the remote hill community of Lonesome Valley. Blind Hartley and his wife competed successfully with the horse traders and Salvation Army singers on a street corner for the attention of passers-by in the county-seat courthouse square as they sang the old ballads to fiddle and guitar accompaniment; but it was Blind Frailey with his lonesome violin that the hill people expected to fiddle his way right through the "golden gates of Heaven."

More abundant in Stuart's writings than his mention of songs have been his accounts of mountain dances and fiddle tunes, such as "Chicken Reel," "Cripple Creek," "Sourwood Mountain," "Leather Breeches," "Zeb Turner's Gal," "The Turkey Scratch" (breakdown)—and especially "Birdie," which a Stuart character called "the best dance tune that ever come from a mountain fiddle." The dances include "Cage the Bird," "Figure Eight," "Grapevine Twist," and others known wherever square dancing has become popular. Fiddles, banjos, and guitars made music for the frolics while someone with a clear, loud voice *called*. The caller, as present-day callers do, improvised the *patter* to make the calls fit the company and the occasion.

At a mountain *bellin'* of newlyweds where the whisky flowed freely among the men and boys the *calls* included the following rollicking stanzas:

I take my licker
And I take it straight,
Grab your Honey
And pat her down eight.

Groundhog leather
Snead without a blade,
All hands together
And let's promenade.

Hickory log and a poplar stump,
Hold in the floor and everybody jump,
Sashaway to the right and don't get wrong,
Meet your Honey and promenade around.

First couple out and circle four.
Right hands crossed and circle four—
Left hands crossed and circle four
And step right through the old side door.

Opposite partners swing and waltz around
Now swing your partner and waltz again—
Swing 'em right and don't get wrong
And meet your Honey and waltz her around.

Swing Little Susie and Mary Ann
Hurry up Daisy Bee. Don't leave your man.

CAGE THE BIRD

First couple out and circle.
Cage that bird, that purty little bird,

Bird hops out and the crow hops in,
All hands up and gone again.

Move, children, move! Move, children, move!
Too slow that step you're in!
Move, children, move! Move, children, move!

Change left-hand lady, left hand around,
Partner by the right and go whirly-giggin' round.

You swing yours and I'll swing mine,
El mend your left—

Meet your Honey and go right and left—
Sift the meal and save the bran,
I'm goin' home with Sally Ann—

GRAPEVINE TWIST

Jine hands and circle down south
Git that sunshine in your mouth.

Chickens in the barnyard pickin' up corn,
The Devil's goin' to git you shore's you're born.

Turn them corners, turn them slow,
Maybe the last time, I don't know.
Ho by-gosh and ho by-joe!
First couple out and lady in the lead,
Gent falls through and takes the lead.
Lady falls through the old side door,
Swing in the center and tie up four,
You tie up four in the center of the floor.
Left-hand lady and left-hand dough,
Partner to the right and go waltz the floor.

Swing the one that stole the sheep.
Now swing the one that stole the meat,
Now the one that gnawed the bone,
Now the one you left at home.

Everybody swing!

Swing and balance two,
Git that lady behind you!

All home and dance your best.
What air you goin' to do,
With your elbow left.
Watch 'em come and watch 'em go,
And watch 'em shake that calico.

Meet your partner and promenade!
Everybody swing!

Circle four in the middle of the floor,
Left-hand lady go left hand around,
Meet your honey as she comes round,
Around behind and swing when you meet,
Back to the center, and oh, how sweet!

Everybody swing!

Figure Eight

First couple out—change and swing.
Croquet waltz and croquet swing.
Change right back to the same old thing,
Croquet waltz and croquet swing.
Circle four, left-hand lady and left-hand dough,
Partner by the right and waltz the floor.

Jump up high and come down straight.
Sixteen hands and circle eight,
Circle eight when you git straight.
Knock down Sall and pick up Kate.

Everybody swing!

Move, children, move!
Move, children, move!

She went up the new cut road,
And I come down the lane,
Stuck my toe in a holler log
And out jumped Lizzie Jane.

Meet your Honey with a double hook-on,
And promenade your own.

In *Taps for Private Tussie,* while the Tussies were living life to the hilt and enjoying spending Kim Tussie's $10,000 life-insurance money, nightly square dances kept the whole neighborhood aroused. Mott and Uncle George played "Sallie Goodin," "Hell Among the Yearlings," "Susie Ann," and the ubiquitous "Birdie." The boy Sid Tussie remarks that Grandpa wouldn't work because of his weak back, but he could dance and call figures loud enough to be heard a mile away. He could crack his heels together three times before he touched the floor.

In *Album of Destiny* Stuart more than once refers to the dance call "Down Yonder," but gives no details of the figures. In poem number 133 of *Man with a Bull-Tongue Plow* he speaks of "Waltz the Hall" as the "most Kentuckian of all dance calls." And in even more enthusiastic terms in "The Bellin of the Bride": "Got the old Kentucky 'Waltz the Hall' in their blood and they'll never get it out. . . . They'll dance right through the pearly gates and up to God on His throne."

Dances, or indoor singing and skipping games accompanied sometimes by clapping, were usually called *plays* inside and *games* outside. These dance-games, such as "Skip to My Lou," and nondancing party games, usually "kissing games," were both popular at hill parties. In "A Yard of String" Stuart deviated from the typical use of such games among younger people and used them in an adult gathering of married couples—probably not typical. The basic game of *Fine and Superfine,* involving redeeming pawns by forfeits, usually became a kissing game.

If Kentucky hill parties have tended to become at mid-century a gathering place for sophisticated *town folk* and if hill people nowadays sometimes prefer watching and listening to the "Grand Old Opry" from Nashville, Tennessee rather than the more strenuous participation in hill dances and games, Stuart leaves no doubt of the key place such parties held in the earlier culture of his community.

Playground games have a place in Stuart's writings—
London Bridge, Fox and Dog, Needle's Eye. The last named
provides the framework and theme for Stuart's book on
mountain education, *The Thread That Runs So True*. It is a
game song with a catchy rhythm:

> The needle's eye that does supply
> The thread that runs so true,
> Many a beau have I let go
> Because I wanted you.
>
> Many a dark and stormy night
> When I went home with you,
> I'd stump my toe and down I'd go
> Because I wanted you.

he described the game, as played by the children of Lonesome Valley School:

> . . . They had formed a circle, hand in hand, and around
> and around they walked and sang these words while two
> pupils held their locked hands high for the circle to pass
> under. Suddenly the two standing—one inside the circle
> and one outside—let their arms drop down to take a pupil
> from the line. Then the circle continued to march and
> sing while the two took the pupil aside and asked him
> whether he'd rather be a train or an automobile.

The game usually ended with a tug of war between those
who chose the train and those who chose the automobile
(or whatever the choice might have been).

For *London Bridge* two girls would stand facing each
other, clasping each other's hands, held high, while the other
girls and boys formed a circle and marched under the arch
of their uplifted hands as they sang, "London Bridge is falling down" and "Build it up with sticks and stones." The two
pairs of arms of the London Bridge would close on a boy or

girl from the circle, and the two girls would take him out to one side and ask his sweetheart's name.

Boys' games that usually were too fast or too rough for the girls were *Fox and Dog* and *Buckeyes*. The former was an imitation fox chase, with the fastest runner holding the honored title of *Fox*. The *Hounds* sometimes chased the *Fox* over meadows, through woods, and down hollows during the entire lunch hour on school days. Of the latter, Stuart recalls in *The Year of My Rebirth:*

> Big Aaron Howard, who could throw a buckeye like a bullet, Little Ed, Glen, and I used to get into a buckeye fight out in some open pasture field where we could see and have plenty of room to get out of the way of one that had smoke on it. "Playing buckeyes," we called it. When one of us got hit, he had to leave the fight. Usually he wanted to leave it anyway after he got hit. I've been knocked down with many a buckeye Big Aaron threw. He was a baseball pitcher in later years.

As in his recording of song texts, Stuart has given only incidental attention to instructions for party, playground, and floor games. He has recorded enough, however, to show that the hill children as well as their elders were resourceful in adapting their pleasures as well as other phases of their living to the native environment, and he has shown beyond doubt that older traditional games have survived in their midst. Although his texts and sets of detailed instructions are not numerous, Stuart has referred to the old songs, square dances, and games frequently enough to show his appreciation of them and to show the basic part they played in the hill culture of his early life.

Of more significance to Stuart's interpretation of the hill mind than his accounts of mountain songs and games have been his ubiquitous references to the supernatural. In additon to the concretely envisioned concepts of Heaven, Hell,

God, and the Devil, Stuart has presented a characteristic sampling of interpretations of birthmarks and other *judgments*, death warnings and other omens, death embodiments, both friendly and unfriendly ghosts, devil tales, evidences of witchcraft, and religious legends.

Stuart implies several areas of rationalization, but makes it clear that people of his land in his life and time have fully believed in supernatural manifestations. Marvelous happenings may have been most frequent among the *Forty-Gallon Baptists* or others who thought it no defilement of the *temple of clay* to enjoy pure mountain whisky. The vividness of the hill preachers' descriptions of Hell during revival *altar calls* and their encouragement of trance-like visions did nothing to discourage such visitations. Where medical facilities were so inadaquate, a serious illness or accident in itself might serve as a convincing death *token*. Wishful thinking, as well as guilt feelings, perhaps produced strong illusions. But the most powerful factor at work, aided by all of the foregoing, was probably the primitive tendency of an unschooled folk to explain all phenomena in terms they could accept and understand.

Birthmarks, from the hill man's and hill woman's point of view, were never the result of chance: they might result from a pregnant mother's unsatisfied craving for a certain food, from a frightening or unpleasant experience of the mother; or they might be a sign of sin visited upon the children unto remote generations of the person committing the original sin. The mother's fright during the rescue of her husband from a snake caused the baby Frons to be born with "the prints of the prettiest little racer black snake right over his heart." Uncle Op's Brother Adger was marked on the cheek by a lizard, a little gray scaly stripe. Sister Fain Groan's harelip (marked by a rabbit?) and her patch of *sow-belly* skin on her arm she considered to be marks that she must bear "for the sins" of her people. In "Toes" a woman's cruel laughter at a man's mashed toes marks the seventh child of each forthcoming generation with *duck feet*, or webbed toes. A man's red face shows he was marked with a turkey when a gobbler flogged his mother at the corncrib one morning. A scandalous mark of the Devil himself—a baby with a long tail and two little horns on its forehead—was rumored in Blakesburg to be evidence enough that the parents had been in league with the Devil.

Certain circumstances, situations, and events were called *judgments*, or demonstrations of God's anger against man for sinning. In the short story "Braska Comes Through," a woman's suffering from guilt feelings and her inability to *come through* when she tried to *give herself to God* were interpreted as punishment for her earlier refusal to bear children that she had conceived. Only after she had borne a child, at the age of forty-four, was she able to overcome the curse and *see the light*.

These consequences of sin have nearly always been involved with humor in Stuart's stories. Old Man Eversole, after an evil life on earth, has become the man in the moon for mountain boys to empty their revolvers at, out of high good spirits; but a vestige of an old folk motif lingers amid the humor. In "Death Has Two Good Eyes," Uncle Melvin's disgraceful death in his "unlawful second wife's" *privy* also suggests a resemblance to ancient belief—that a humiliating death is a fit punishment for adultery.

In *The Good Spirit of Laurel Ridge*, Old Op, who can never be trusted not to be telling a straight-faced tall-tale lie, explained to city Alf that it was safe to go to the town of Honeywell only if one were *right with Him on High:*

". . . A long time ago when Pap was a boy, there was a break clear out to Lonesome Hill—that's the Honeywell Graveyard. It went out from Big River in the shape of an oxbow and then went back to Big River. All of Honeywell was inside that break. It was so deep ye couldn't see the bottom. I've heard people could walk up and look down and sniff the brimstone" [from Hell, of course!].

"That break closed up in a single night. . . . And fer a long time atter that, the merchants in that town started treatin' the country people right. . . . That town is jist a-sittin' there on a ledge of ground with all the underpinnin' gone. The Master can spring the trap any time. He's warned 'em by lettin' the bottoms fall from their wells. It's a token."

In *Plowshare in Heaven* the explanation of the destruction of the hang tree in "Sunday Afternoon Hanging" clearly derived from religious folk belief involved with magic.

That old tree fell three years ago. . . . Must a been some of them innocent men they swung up there, and in Heaven they got after God Almighty to do something about that tree. . . . Well, of all the trees in the lower end of Blakesburg, the old elm where they hung all them men was the only one the lightnin' hit and split from limb to roots. Tree must have been five feet through the middle, too. And don't you know the people wouldn't burn a stick of that wood in their stoves and fireplaces. . . . People was afraid if they burnt it they would be haunted the rest of their days.

Death and mutilation seemed to the hill people a fitting punishment sent upon men for disturbing the dead in "The Word and the Flesh." ("It's against the *Word* to *prank* with the dead.") In "The Storm," when Mom was prevented for the third time from carrying out her plan to leave her husband, she made a final decision not to go: "Third time's the charm for me," she said; and Mick happily accepted her reasoning. In "Rain on Tanyard Hollow" the overwhelming storm that follows Pappy's prayer up in the garden patch (after his confession that the black snake on the fence to bring rain "is a false image, Lord") carried religion into the realm of magic.

Witchcraft dominated "The Sanctuary Desolated": Grandma did not wish to live in her daughter's house; once there, she insisted upon an unobstructed view of her own ramshackle house. First, she had to have water carried from her own well; then she urged her son-in-law to cut his young rye crop between her house and his, and when he refused a storm laid the crop flat without affecting anything else; next, she wanted a flowering apple tree cut down, and when her son-in-law refused, a storm uprooted *that tree* and nothing else. A few months later, in her own home, she sent her grandchildren to safety during a storm, and was killed by the falling oak tree everyone had warned her would fall on the house someday—died, the story implied, in that place and manner by her own wish.

All of Stuart's forthright references to witchcraft are associated with the Sutton family. Esmerelda's two old-maid aunts were credited with bewitching men, cattle, sheep, and hogs. Men in the neighborhood were sure that Aunt Phoeby prevented them from unearthing a pot of gold believed to be buried on Warfield Flaugherty's "pint above the sycamore bottom"; the dirt fell back into the holes faster than the men could shovel it out, and at one spot a big two-headed bull (head and pair of horns on each end) walked right up a certain pine tree.

Esmerelda herself concentrated her *fitifying* powers on one man and his hounds and stock—Jake Hunt, her old sweetheart and future husband. Jake put himself in her power by giving her money for a cow and accepting from her the gift of many kisses: ". . . My bull wouldn't notice my cows. My cows wouldn't give their milk down. My mules stood on their hind feet and tried to walk like men." On one occasion, at the crucial moment in a fox hunt, she was credited with having transformed all the dogs into foxes and the tired old fox into a hound. (Jake meanwhile tried to stand on his head on the stopper of his whisky jug, although he was not a man "to hanker after licker.") Lute Puckett reported to him that he had overheard Esmerelda bargaining with the Devil up in the cemetery to get Jake for her husband, offering her soul to return for her heart's desire. Jake knew that he had to take action: He melted a fifty-cent piece into a silver bullet, unearthed from the bottom of an old trunk a picture of Esmerelda as a beautiful young girl, and broke the Devil's power over her by shooting her picture with the silver bullet, making her a fit woman to be his wife. Gone forever was the *mean look* from her beautiful brown eyes, and gone forever was the invisible (to all except Esmerelda) little brown mouse familiar that had been the Devil's agent. Here, as in so much of Stuart's writing dealing with the supernatural, humor holds sway.

The parents of the devil-marked baby confessed in a Holiness revival their sins of trafficking with the Devil, and were ready to go straight to Heaven when they mistook the aurora borealis for the Judgment Day; but the baby's grave continued to be the Devil's territory: ". . . anybody in Blakesburg will tell you if you go into the patch of woods where this devil-marked baby is buried that it will start thundering and lightning and the rain will start pouring. Many people have tried it. . . ." Reece Nimrod, who made the discovery, knew the storm was the Devil's work, for less than a quarter of a mile from the grave he reached sunshine and dry ground.

Fate, religion, witchcraft, and luck have been close relatives in hill thinking. The signs and predictions have far more often pointed to bad luck, danger, and death than to good fortune; and dire misfortunes were expected if one broke a tabu, religious or otherwise.

Among the few good-luck signs Stuart has mentioned are saving the first lamb of the season (good luck for the whole season) and finding one's initials in a spiderweb (make a wish and it will come true).

The hill woman's way of looking into the future that Stuart referred to in several stories was by *reading the coffee grounds:* after she had finished drinking her coffee, she turned the cup upside down to drain, and read the design left by the dregs in the bottom of the cup. In "A Land Beyond the River" Mom saw wealth for her daughters but death for her son. Arn Sparks in *Hie to the Hunters* saw "misery, trouble, and death" shortly before an attempt was made to burn the barn with two sleeping boys in the loft. The anxious mother in "Bury Your Dead," whose weakly son had married into a slave-driving feuding family, saw a coffin every morning in the coffee grounds left in her cup.

Bad-luck signs other than death warnings and weather lore have included seeing a hoot owl fly over one at night and seeing a gray fox in the cornfield. Several tabus related to plants and animals: do not set a hen in dog days (the chickens will die); do not burn owl feathers (bad luck among the chickens for seven years); do not kill a toad-frog (the cows will give bloody milk); do not burn a sassafras tree (bad luck); do not let anyone sweep around you if you expect to be married soon (you will not marry). Battle Keaton's third wife's fear of crossing a stream may also have been involved with superstition.

A few bad-luck signs were associated with physical characteristics, such as for a man's hair to have two crowns (sign of a potential murderer), to be *narrow between the eyes,* or to have a *simelon head* (signs of low intelligence).

Stuart made a very personal application of the superstition associating bad luck with Friday the thirteenth: he and Naomi Deane Norris postponed their wedding until five minutes after midnight to avoid the bad-luck stigma of the day they had inadvertently chosen.

Stuart's writings reflect the widespread credence given by

the hill people to warnings, or *tokens,* of danger and death: dreams, visions, voices in the wind, ghostly apparitions, animal behavior are often interpreted as divine revelations. Only good men and women were likely to get death tokens that would enable them to set their affairs in order, but sinners sometimes had dreams—medieval in their concreteness—as warnings to change their ways before it was too late.

Bird behavior has been almost universally interpreted as a death warning, as in the following memorial verse to a soldier:

> A bird flew in
> At th' head o' my bed. . . .
> It told me that
> My Jim was dead. . . .
> I knew the sign of warning.

A woman whose husband worked away from home in a West Virginia coal mine expressed a similar belief:

> I got uneasy when a whippoorwill
> Came on the porch last night. That is a sign
> Death takes one of the house. . . .

The sight of mules riding each other and the sound of dogs howling were considered death portents.

Throughout the Kentucky highlands, at least into the 1930s, there were people who believed that it was an invitation to death to transplant a cedar tree—that the person who moved it would die as soon as the tree grew large enough to shelter a grave.

In "Dark Winter" Mom's dream, following her natural anxiety for a frail infant ("the least baby I ever saw"), was interpreted as a token, for the child died soon thereafter: ". . . I dreamed last night that Mitchell played with a lot of babies up there on the hill under that oak tree. I couldn't climb the hill to get him. I had to stay at the foot and watch him." Grandpa Tussie's dream of burned new ground, of ashes and hopeless efforts to find a mountain path among the charred stumps were convincing death tokens. When he heard the voices of his parents calling him, he forgave his enemies, stopped working on his house, and went to bed with the certainty of going to Heaven. Old Doug Grayhouse heard the *death bells* just before he died. One of the old men in "300 Acres of Elbow Room" had heard it said that tokens "told people things": ". . . They come like headless men or in the forms of light, and they speak to people. I've heard of them comin' in the form of a shepherd dog at night or a pig that run across the road and squealed." In the same story Big Eif Porter's token foretold the exact hour of death. Not only Big Eif but "his Pap and his Pap's Pap" were similarly warned of the exact hour of death, and "changed worlds at the appointed time." Even fearless Uncle Uglybird drank less moonshine after he saw the Devil down by the railroad tracks in Blakesburg. He said that the experience was some sort of token, but he "hadn't been able to figure out what kind."

One of the poems in *Man with a Bull-Tongue Plow* interprets a small incident as a death warning. Twice when the speaker in the poem got a paper to wipe his razor while he was shaving, "that paper cut a caper" and floated out of the house to stop beside his son's grave.

Peg Sparks had an elaborate dream token, corroborating his wife's reading in the coffee grounds, of a barn burning in *Hie to the Hunters* that would have destroyed Did and Sparkie if the family had not heeded the warning and stayed on the alert. Peg was a *seventh son of the third generation,* and had the power of seeing ghosts and having visions: ". . . And when the flame shot up toward the stars and God blew it out with a great puff of His breath, I looked down where the barn had once stood and . . . it was a pile of cold ashes. . . ."

In many stories Stuart has attributed to old hill men the perception of a concrete embodiment of death, as they become aware of the nearness of their own dying. A buzzard, a spider, a bull black snake sometimes has seemed to be functioning merely as a symbol; but in at least one story, "When Mountain Men Make Peace," Death was perceived as a physical presence in the form of a buzzard. "Death can be anything when he wants a man," said Mel Renfroe:

> ". . . Day before yesterday, when it thundered and lightened, Death was a turkey buzzard a-ridin' high on the wind before the storm. . . .
>
> "Yesterday . . . Death was a beardy-faced man dressed in ragged clothes, holding to that barbed-wire fence up there on the bank. . . .
>
> "Today's the third day and he might reach me. . . . He's liable to come in the form of a bull black snake crawlin' across the yard to get the wren that builds on the kitchen porch. He's liable to be a water-soaked stranger that runs into this house from a storm. But I think Death will be back today in the form of a turkey buzzard."

So sure is Mel that these things betoken his imminent death that he confesses all his sins so that he can "look Him in the eye." As he dies, his son Creech exclaims, "Lord Almighty, that buzzard swooped low!"

In the same story is a hint of revenants in bird form. Mel's friend Ceif Salyers had killed three *revenooers;* Mel had no guilt on his conscience for the killings, but felt compelled to urge Ceif to make his peace about the murders before his own time to die. Ceif tried to brush aside his guilt feelings, but just then: ". . . he saw three streaks of lightning in the sky, and when the lightning flashed again he thought he saw three large birds flying high above the treetops. . . ." He angrily denied belief that the birds were the *revenooers*. The young narrator in "Betwixt Life and Death" wondered if the soul of his dead grandpa had returned in the form of the little screech owl flying about the place. Old Op Akers rather planned to return to Laurel Ridge as a chicken hawk after his death, for he was sure that those numbered among the blessed would be permitted to return to a place as beloved as Laurel Ridge had always been to him. Some people he wanted to frighten by "a-flutterin' against their winderpanes at night," and he wanted to float over some of them "like a big chicken hawk, pumpin' my wings." In "Grandpa Birdwell's Last Battle" was a suggestion of the revenant in snake form. The copperhead that the old man trampled to death in the *entry* had "the countenance of Bill Sexton," a dead enemy; and Grandpa, who survived the copperhead bites, at last felt content at having evened the score with the only man who had ever *whipped* him in mortal life.

In *The Year of My Rebirth*, Stuart noted the falling away of superstition in W-Hollow, and expressed regret that his own childhood fear of ghosts kept him from seeing the lights and hearing the whirring of wings at the Peddler's Well. "The great tall tales about this place have flown with the winds of yesteryear." Since Esmerelda Sutton was the last witch that even Old Op "had heard tell of around here," witches seem to have become even scarcer than ghosts. Stuart's stories reflect abundantly, however, a widespread belief of past generations in the free roaming of spirits along the hollows and ridges of his neighborhood.

The ghostly ore diggers and "twelve yoke of oxen a-pullin' a big-wheeled wagon loaded with charcoal" and other ghosts of men killed on Laurel Ridge were reportedly seen by fox hunters of several generations. These stories, usually told by the old men such as Op Akers and Uncle Uglybird, have suggested nostalgia for the days when

Laurel Ridge was a flourishing community with the big Six
Hickories Church, more than a hundred houses, seventeen
iron furnaces, and a ridge road crowded with horse-drawn
and oxen-drawn vehicles. According to legend, a woodchop-
per firing the brush to kill the snakes on his place set a fire
that went *fast as a horse could run* and devastated the
whole area of both its houses and its timber, forcing the
people to settle elsewhere, and leaving behind a ghost-
infested wasteland.

Another Laurel Ridge ghost story growing out of historical legend carried a suggestion of the revengeful revenant
motif. Old Op related this tale of the ghostly aftermath of
Civil War days guerrilla fighting:

> ". . . many a night I've heard the sound of hosses'
> hoofs a-poundin' this Laurel Ridge road. . . . I've
> jumped from my bed and run to the door, opened it in a
> hurry and looked up and down the road and never saw a
> man or a hoss. . . . It's General Morgan and his Cavalry.
> Back there at that arc on Laurel Ridge, down behind the
> big rocks, the old men and boys stopped 'im onct and
> made 'im turn tail when he was a-goin' to raid Ohio in the
> days of the Rebellion. . . . But Morgan got out of that
> death trap in a hurry. Carried away his dead and
> wounded. Don't know how many men were kilt. Don't
> know where he buried his dead. But they come back here
> and worry me since I'm the son of George Akers, who hid
> behind a rock with a long rifle and helped stop 'em.
> . . ."

Eddie Birchfield, the Pied Piper of Blakesburg, had a
store of ghost tales, including one of a ghostly milkwoman
milking a ghostly cow near a house in Shinglemill Hollow:

> . . . a woman who had once lived there and had milked a
> cow so many times with a little shawl around her shoul-
> ders . . . he had seen her fifty years after her death with

the same shawl around her shoulders at the spot where the milkgap used to be . . . and he said he saw with his own eyes streams of milk going into her tin pail and he heard the stream zigzag across the bottom of the bucket. . . . He said when he spoke to the woman she faded on the wind and was no more.

Eddie also told of seeing a big red ghost dog climb up on the same house and tear off shingles with its mouth: ". . . when he called to the dog, he ran through the air like a dog runs on the ground. He said he could hear the dog's feet hitting the wind until the dog was out of sight."

Also harmless were the hitchhiking ghosts of young Rinda Stevens and Tom Kitchen, drowned on the eve of their wedding, who appeared to have had a ghostly ceremony, according to Old Op:

". . . One Sunday, back when Teddy Roosevelt was President, old Doc Burton drove his two-hoss surrey out Laurel Ridge to see Mort Doore. . . . On his way back, a young couple walked outten Six Hickories Church House. Doc Burton didn't know the young couple who flagged 'im fer a ride. They said they were on their way to Honeywell. The young woman was dressed in white and was carryin' a armload of flowers. . . . Said he talked to the couple till he started down Seaton Hollow. . . . When he drove into Honeywell and turned to ast 'em where they wanted out, they were gone, nothin' but the flowers on the back seat."

Old Doc passed out *cold as a cucumber* when he learned that his passengers, who had told him their names, had been drowned at Sandy Falls in the days of President Garfield.

Like a charm was Mom's recurrent midnight trip to the old vacant Garthee house before her children were born: she hoped that the benevolent ghosts of a young couple that

she admired during their lifetime would come out of the
house and walk in the moon shadows "and bring good luck
to her unborn child."

In "Whip-Poor-Willie" Stuart has sketched the background story of the headless woman ghost that recurs in his
writings:

> . . . A woman lived here once, as the story goes, and she
> had a mean husband—so she fixed her little children
> . . . and her lazy man a good dinner and went upstairs,
> tied a sheet around her neck and to the bedpost and
> jumped out the winder. . . . Now a headless woman can
> be seen here at this house—and something that goes like
> all the dishes falling out'n the safe—something like a wolf
> on the roof has been seen with a big mouth and white
> teeth tearing off the shingles.

Elsewhere Stuart associated both the headless woman ghost
and the dog ghost with the site of his present home in W-
Hollow, and added the apparition of a small child seen flying around the house on a pair of white wings.

Stuart's most frequently recurring ghost, that of headless
old peddler Nick, recalls a legend of robbery and murder.
Although no one really knows the truth, "our grandsires
told our sires and they told us" that three young men
robbed the old peddler, murdered him, and threw his body
and his broken-up buggy into the well:

> This lone headless peddler going out at night.
> Sol Spraddling saw him headless in his buggy.
> Sol said that he was driving in a hurry.
> The sight that T. L. Shelton saw was worse—
> Met headless Nick a-leading home his horse—
> And children claim they've seen Nick cross the road
> And on his back was strapped a heavy load.
> The old men who have lived close said they heard

The cracks of heavy whips and drivers' words,
And when they looked they saw an empty road.

Another ghostly light was mentioned in connection with the
house in Shinglemill Hollow, a big light that some saw several times as it fell recurrently beside a certain locust tree.
By Stuart's boyhood the supernatural manifestations had less
definite forms and were chiefly lights and whirring sounds,
as of wings.

A comic touch appears in some accounts of the woman
ghost who haunted only men slow to marry. This ghost was
linked by legend with the suicide of a jilted woman, who
returned in the best ballad tradition to haunt her false
lover. Did hears the story in *Hie:*

> "I've heard people say that she lived in the old shack
> that stood near that well. . . . Said she was supposed to
> marry a man that lived in Lonesome Cove. . . . Said the
> man jilted 'er and she jumped into the well and ended 'er
> own life. Now she spends all her eternity a-skeerin' the
> life outen the Plum Grove men that are slow to git mar-
> ried, that go with girls too long or that wrong the girls
> they go with."

This beautiful white-robed ghost snatched men's caps as
they passed the oxbow turn in the Shackle Run jolt-wagon
road or walked a little way with them—but never appeared
to them again after they had married.

Another ghost yarn, made credible by guilt and drink,
appeared in "Moonin' Round the Mountain." Moonshine-
loving Ace Hatfield *sparked* Treecy for fourteen years,
but she would not marry him while he drank. One night on
his way home past the Short Branch Graveyard, he heard
and saw the wandering ghost of his whisky-drinking father,
"bounded by the ground plane" and "tied to this old world"
because of his past sins. Ace's horse reared as his father's

white-bearded ghost blocked the way, wearing the black suit he was buried in and making movements that were characteristic of him in life. Ace emptied his pistols at this apparition, driving it back to its grave.

Stuart also exploits for humor the old motif of superstitious anxiety, if not actual belief, that ill luck would befall one who ignored deathbed requests:

> "You know Old Bennie Wellkid before he died ast that they bury him in a hollow-black-gum log—just poke him down in it feet-first and nail some boards over the end of the log." . . . "They talk about diggin' him up and buryin' him that way yet." . . . "He's hanted them. They think he has. A man has been seen run across the road several times nigh the place where they buried Bennie."

Like Ace Hatfield, Tom Wellkid threatened to fill the annoying ghost with bullet holes, further illustrating the persistent confusion of spirit with flesh and blood which Stuart attributed to himself as a child and to his more old-fashioned characters of all ages.

The fear of passing graveyards alone at night was one of the most prevalent indications of the hill man's belief in ghosts, and one of the many illustrations in Stuart's writings of the hill folk's paradoxical belief that the soul went at once to Heaven or Hell and at the same time that it remained with the body, or near it.

All Stuart's references to knocking spirits seem to have their inception in one local legend of the murder of an old Indian medicine man, believed to have had somewhere a buried treasure—"just white sheets of silver running through bright panels of gold . . . like the streets of Heaven." The only verifiable part of the legend was that a medicine man who wore his black hair in a long pigtail and had a headdress of feathers spent a week in Jimpson Burr selling liver remedies and hair tonic and pulling old snaggle teeth with his bare hands. The legend held that money-mad men killed Red Jacket when he refused to disclose the whereabouts of his hidden treasure, that the murderers hid the body under some tree branches in the Widow Skaggs' hog lot, that the body was rooted out by hogs and hounds and the bones picked clean by the crows.

Notwithstanding this tale of horror, Red Jacket's spirit bore little resemblance to the revengeful revenant. In "Red Jacket: the Knockin' Sperit," his activities were involved with those of a medium who, like Op Akers, was a seventh child of a seventh generation, and consequently able to see and commune with the spirits of the dead. To some extent the visions and voices are rationalized by the presence of Ada Bee Sizemore wearing a white flowing robe and appearing and disappearing behind a screen. In this story the spirits seemed more concerned with exposing unfaithful husbands and wives and convincing doubters of the reality of spirits than in any tangible revenge upon the men who had wronged them personally. Although the rough capers of the medium's table (presumably the work of Red Jacket) were left in the realm of mystery, the over-all effect of this story was broad humor, not awe.

The treasure was never found. If such a treasure ever existed "it still remains hidden in an old pantry, under a floor, under some leaves, in a cave, or an abandoned coal mine."

In *The Good Spirit of Laurel Ridge* Red Jacket seems to have become dissociated from the lost-treasure story and to have become an ally of Old Op in driving off undesirable city intruders from Laurel Ridge. Op explains that Red Jacket used to be an Indian chief, but that he has become a leader of the knocking spirits that will knock on the head of a bed, on an ax handle, or even a hatband; he will climb the wall and "come down with eyes like balls of fire." He describes them as becoming a nuisance, but as non-malevolent—resembling household familiars, more playful than frightening or awe-inspiring.

A semireligious etiological tale that Stuart has attributed to the Leadinghams lacks the artistry of the true folk tale but contains the ancient motifs of invisibility and supernatural kindness. Aunt Nancy Leadingham, who told the story in 1916, traced it back through three generations:

> "Once there was a family of poor children who looked up at the sky and cried for the stars. . . . Suddenly a stranger just came from nowhere dressed in a high hat and a Prince Albert suit, and asked the children why they were crying. 'Because we want the stars up there so high and beautiful,' said one. . . . 'Well, since you have such lofty ambition to look toward Heaven and want the most beautiful thing in the world, I will do all I can to help you get the stars. . . . If they won't come down to you, I will fix it so you can bend down to them.'
>
> "Then, Pap told us, the stranger disappeared quicker than the flash of an eye. . . . Then one of the children looked down at the green spring grass, and everywhere there in the light of the stars they could see the shining lumps of gold . . . of dandelions, a flower never known before the children had cried for the stars."

Aunt Nancy could not recall the "happy song" that her father had sung about the children who wished for the stars and found them at their feet.

Probably Old Op fabricated the explanation of the morning mist rising in the hills: ". . . the groundhogs are making their coffee. . . . When ye see clouds a-hangin' over the valleys. . . . That's the steam from their coffee bilers, the old people allus told me."

Stuart recalled that during his childhood the family observed Old Christmas as the birthday of Christ:

Our mother and father told us that on January 7 the violets bloomed again under last year's leaves and the snow. They told us that the mountain daisy and often the apple, peach, pear would bloom. When I was a child, I searched for proof of these things. . . .

My mother and father said that the fox wouldn't catch the birds and the dog wouldn't harm the rabbits on Old Christmas. . . .

Another beautiful legend of love had it that on this night all animals could speak to each other in the same language and understand each other. . . .

We children used to wonder in what language the animals spoke to each other and what they said. . . .

Here Stuart combines an old and widely diffused legend with his love of nature in the Kentucky hill setting.

Other facets of the folk mind and adaptation to the hill environment appear in Stuart's recording of weather lore, planting customs, herb and power medicine, and other miscellaneous beliefs relating to the hill setting.

When a hill man said *it's a sure sign,* he had great faith in his predictions; and his accuracy in predicting the weather has sometimes proved to have a scientific basis. The croaking of *rain crows* (yellow-billed cuckoos), the owls hooting *lonesome-like* in the afternoon, and the lonely cries of wild geese heading South predicted bad weather; but the bittern's cry, according to the old men, meant that cold days were over. When leaves turned "their soapy bellies to the wind and hot sun," when there were red clouds at morning, when there was a circle around the moon, the old-timers prepared for bad weather. Glen Hilton advised Jesse Stuart not to buy strawberry plants on one occasion because the "spiderwebs everywhere" meant a long, dry spell. When mules and horses ran in the pasture and kicked up their heels, it was a sign of bad weather. Little mare-tail clouds were considered a rain sign in "The Storm." (Grandpa Tussie quoted a common saying of the hill people when he said, "All signs fail in dry weather.") In *Beyond Dark Hills*, little white clouds about the size of a duck's feather were a sure sign of drought. Chickens going to roost and martins hurrying to their boxes at midday were sure signs of rain. Smoke blowing toward the ground foretold rain, or *falling weather*.

Several times repeated was the belief that rabbits prophesy the number of snows during a winter by the number of circles they gnaw around the sassafras stems and the depth of the deepest snow by the number of inches high they gnaw on the stems. A black Christmas was considered the sign of a poor crop year; a white Christmas, the sign of a good crop year. A rainy June was also a bad crop sign; a dry June, a good sign. A different aspect of weather lore was illustrated by Anse Bushman's going out into the spring equinoctial storm: "If I git a soakin now, I can git wet any time this year and it won't hurt me."

Stuart's farmers have not agreed completely on their crop lore: one white-bearded farmer planted his corn in the dark of the moon:

> ". . . so hit won't grow tall and will have big ears. And I plant my 'taters in the light of the moon so they'll grow nigh the top of the ground and will be easy to dig! And I kiver my buildin's with clapboards in the dark of the moon so they won't curl up at the ends. . . ."

Old Op planted his *'taters* in the dark of the moon in late March, considering that the proper time to plant root vegetables so they would not all go to vines. Rufus Litteral, who grew the biggest potatoes in Blakesburg, had learned from his grandmother to do things by the zodiac. In "Dark Winter" Pop says the time to plant potatoes is in the light of the moon so they will grow big and at the top of the ground and be easy to dig. Grandpa Tussie disagreed with the character in *Foretaste of Glory* as to the proper time for nailing boards on the house, believing they will curl in the dark of the moon (this contradiction can probably be resolved by noting the fact that green wood will usually curl, no matter whether the moon is waxing or waning at the time the carpentry takes place). Farmers in the area worked hard to cut sprouts from their pastures during "dog days," believing that during that time "they bleed to death and rot out of the ground."

A grimmer application of the old superstition that things sink into the ground in the dark of the moon occurs in "Sunday Afternoon Hanging" when the Sixeymores murder old Jim Murphy and his wife "and throwed them in Sandy in the dark of the moon," thinking "the bodies would never come to the top of the water."

Among the bits of miscellaneous animal lore that Stuart has mentioned are these: if a turtle gets hold of a person he won't let go until it thunders, or until the sun sets; horsehairs left in water nine days will turn into snakes; snakes go blind in dog days.

Herb or *yarb* medicine has been widely practiced in Stuart's region, as in other sections of the highlands. "There's a weed a-growin' on Laurel Ridge for every ailment of the body," said Old Op Akers with conviction. Op chewed calamus root for his blood pressure, as his father and grandfather had done before him: "Some Indian chief down in North Carolina told my grandpa Powhatan Akers about it." Op boiled roots, barks, and leaves to make himself spring and autumn tonics, and sweetened them with wild honey. He chewed spignet roots in the spring because they "put pounds on ye." Ginseng—rarely dug for home consumption —Op considered good for the heart, either raw or in a tonic. *Sassafrilla* (sarsaparilla) he took "for the blood" and boiled pokeberry root "to fetch soreness from yer body."

Snakeroot seems to have been the aspirin of the hills, which Op and others considered good for colds, chills, and fevers. "Bile the roots and drink the juice," he said. "It's bitter medicine to take but it will do the work." *Bear's paw* was taken "fer the stummick" and yellow root "fer bellyache and sore mouth." *Life everlasting* was the old folks' cure for asthma. Antler seeds of *shoemake* (sumac) boiled with mullein stalks were applied to the throat for quinsy. When poultices of slippery-elm bark and pokeberry root proved less effective than surgery in curing Old Op's cataracts, the experience did not in the least weaken his belief in herb medicine.

Uncle Tid Porter, once "the only doctor in this section" of the hills, gave "spring tonics of slippery-elm bark, shoemake bark, and ginsang and snakeroot." Anse Bushman in *Trees of Heaven* was less specific about the content, but agreed that a good spring tonic of herbs and bark should be boiled "to a bitter gall" to give his "system a good spring cleanin." In "Dark Winter" Pop had faith that he would feel better after taking "a good tonic of wild-cherry bark, may apple, slipper-elm, sassafras, and yellow root boiled together . . . for his constitution." Boneset tea was mentioned in the same context.

Ace Hatfield's mother could not cure his alcoholism with "*yarb* remedies out'n poplar bark, fern roots, wild-cherry bark, yaller root, and the roots of boneset." Nor did the narrator in the following poem have faith in the old remedies:

> Oh, I have done some crazy things at times;
> One time when I was sick and took the tea
> Made of wild-cherry bark, spice-wood, boneset,
> I drank till it was near the death of me.

In "A Bad Disease" Finn was cured of gonorrhea by a doctor's medicine, but his mother recalled earlier remedies for *a bad disease:*

"The doctor back in the mountains told him to eat apples for it. Drink apple juice. Jake et all the green apples in one orchard. It didn't cure him. Old Lum Beaver's yarb remedy was all that done any good. It took four months. . . . Brother Melvin had it a year and was cured by a Faith doctor on Apple Creek. Then he quit laughin' about the sperit's doins."

America in "Woman in the House" used chimney soot to stop the bleeding from a cut made when a man broke a whisky bottle in his hip pocket, and sewed up the *lash* with a darning needle: "I took thirty-seven stitches . . . jist as even as if I'd been tuckin' up a skirt."

Women such as America and Subrinea Tussie in *Trees of Heaven* also served as midwives. America was especially versatile:

"I may not be no doctor, but show me nairy nuther woman that's delivered more babies in this country than I have, and I'll eat her blood raw. Who's cured more sick than I have among cattle and men? Who's cured more colic and fever than I have? Who does the people come to when they want help—even for the drunken fits and blind billiards? . . ."

Other home remedies included Fronnie Bushman's use of groundhog grease for *the rheumaties,* and various treatments for snakebite, such as making a cross-shaped cut across the bite and sucking out the poison, giving whisky and placing a bottle of turpentine to the wound (the green stripes going up in the turpentine bottle indicated that the venom was leaving the wound).

Old Op seems to be combining two or even three traditional *power* cures for snakebite in the second of the following cures, the second being the one he told as a first-person experience: "If Pap had a-given me the black-powder cure,

I'd a-had to've turned my naked starn end to 'im and let 'im a-shot me seven times with cartridges without bullets." Instead, his Pap split a black cat and a black Minarky (Minorca) rooster down the stomach and applied the warm entrails to the bite while the cat and rooster were still kicking. He then lowered Op, with the cat and rooster bandaged to him, into a hole and covered him with dirt well above the navel and left him there for several hours. In context, this cure is a tall tale, greatly embellished.

Also in the realm of power medicine was the cure for *thrash:* having a seventh son or daughter (of a seventh or third generation) blow in the baby's mouth. Related to power medicine was the carrying of charm objects to prevent or relieve disease, such as buckeyes for rheumatism.

Also common as charms were the hanging of a snake on the fence to bring rain and carrying a rabbit's foot for general good luck. Less usual was the incident of the little girls eating bluets and expecting to get their wish of a new dress the color of the flowers.

Water divining is on the wane in the hill country, but *water witches* are not out of business. Battle Keaton with his magic peach-tree forked branch found the vein of water far underground for the well that supplied his family with water for twenty years before his death. Uncle Uglybird Skinner also used the peach-tree fork.

> . . . He disputed with anyone who used the willow fork. He claimed it had failed him but the peach-tree fork had never. He would break a forked branch from a peach tree and hold one of the forks in each hand, letting the main branch be before him. He would walk along and wherever the main fork bent groundward was where he would say there was a vein of water. If it dropped suddenly downward, it was a big vein and not very far down. If it was slow to drop, it was a small vein. He had it all figured out in his head—from the time the fork started

dropping to the place it dropped, was the way he judged the number of feet the diggers would have to dig to hit the vein of water. . . .

Interestingly, this *power* to find veins of water with the help of a forked stick—peach, willow, hazel—has carried no stigma of suspected dealings with the Devil, but has been thought of simply as a gift.

Stuart's creative impulse has been so attuned to the folk traditions of grotesque exaggeration and deadpan delivery that it is sometimes difficult to separate his own creations from his folklore borrowings. The following tall tales, whether of local, family, or wider circulation, almost surely reached Stuart through oral tradition. Naturally, some of them grew out of hill religion. In such a snake-infested setting, it was understandable that many of them would deal with snakes; in so primitive a culture as that of Stuart's W-Hollow boyhood, it was to be expected that tales of strength and size would abound; where lumberjacks have operated, some good imported tales of the Michigan woods have not been surprising. For the most part, local stories predominate here, as they did in the ghost tales.

Stuart referred to Uncle Jarvis Stevenson, former Negro slave, thought to be more than a hundred years old when he died, as "the greatest storyteller ever to live in Blake County"; but he has tapped Uncle Jarvis' story hoard much less than Uncle Op's. Uncle Jarvis' story of wild pigeons "so thick they broke the limbs from the trees" hardly exaggerated historical accounts of those now-extinct Kentucky birds. In the following story Uncle Jarvis used the very old folk motif of the obstacle flight, in which objects are thrown back which the pursuer takes times to pick up.

Sarah Jane Spencer, a white woman who died before Civil War days, was walking to her hill home from Blakesburg with two pairs of shoes and other purchases wrapped up in packages when she became aware of a panther close behind her:

> . . . It was about to catch her and she turned and threw a pair of shoes at it. The hungry panther tore open the box, chewed a minute on each shoe while she ran; then it learned that shoes were not good to eat and that Sarah Jane would be better so it took after her again. When it got close she threw it the second pair of shoes. While it opened the box she ran farther. She threw every package she had to the panther and while it opened them, she ran a bit farther. After she threw the last package she made it to the house. Bill Spencer shot the panther when it came toward the house screaming after his wife who had fallen fallen exhausted on the front steps.

No further sampling is given of the "animal stories" Uncle Jarvis told the children of the town. This one was brought into the modern era by the mention of the panther's having escaped from a show.

Surprisingly few hunting tales have appeared in Stuart's writings. Negro Uncle Jarvis told of a huge fox called Bigfoot that circled as far as fifty miles and lost many of the dogs. Uncle Casper told a tale of Old Tiger MacMeans (who could get down and smell where a fox had been and put the young hounds on a cold trail). One of his blue-tick hounds hung up on a rock cliff: ". . . he blasted rock down with dynamite for eight days and got everybody in the neighborhood to help him get old Queen. . . . She was so nigh gone she couldn't stand up, but when they found her she had the fox right by the tail."

Uncle Casper refers to the war between the fox hunters and the tobacco farmers that broke out as a result of the state law offering a bounty for fox hides (the foxes having become chicken thieves and otherwise a nuisance to farmers), and mentions as a detail that the barn burners could not be caught because they put red pepper on their shoe soles and made the bloodhounds sneeze so that they couldn't follow the trail.

His snake stories were certainly tall tales. In one, a black snake killed a rattlesnake:

> "The snake sorty halted in the garden between two rows of cabbage heads. . . . There was a little patch of briars beside the cabbage patch—in the old fence row beside the garden. That black snake, big around as a baby's leg and long as a rail-fence rider, made a headlong dive into that briar patch like a cat divin' for a mouse. . . .
>
> "That black snake wropped around that big rattler so quick it would make your head swim. Then the black snake started to clampin down with all its strength and bitin the rattler's throat. . . . It whipped it with its tail like it was a buggy whip. The old rattler couldn't take the last beatin. . . .
>
> ". . . It had twenty-seven rattlers and nine buttons. . . . I skinned the rattler and made me a belt out of its hide and Liz a pair of garters."

Another dealt with a racer black snake that he had imprisoned in a knothole in a sourwood sprout by whittling a glut to fit the hole. A year later, when he cut the pole, he found the little tree hollow down to the roots, and "out popped that snake poor as Job's turkey." It remembered him, according to Old Casper, and coiled five times around his ankle "like it was a rope around a well windlass." His wife Liz, noticing that he was "as white as a flour poke," cut the snake with a butcher knife into ten pieces, its teeth still holding the head to his ankle bone.

In "Dawn of Remembered Spring," Mom stuck a potato-digger tine through a big rusty-golden copperhead's skin just enough to pin him to the earth so he could not crawl under the house. By the time Pa came home from work, the snake had thrown so much venom over the ground that weeds would not grow on the spot for four years.

In "The Blue Tick Pig" Mike McGan was credited with telling as firsthand observation the following cow snake story supposed to have taken place a generation earlier:

> ". . . round yonder back of that piney pint, the old cow was pickin up next to a rock cliff and a big cow snake crawled quietly from behind the rock and wound his body up like a corkscrew till he got his mouth over the cow's teat. At first she kicked a little. She mooed and looked at the ground and booed. Then she went on pickin grass and that snake milked every teat she had and then lit right on the other cow and milked her too. And when he got through he was all bloated up and he just rolled up and went to sleep there in the sun. Then Mike said that he shot it . . . right between the eyes and made shoe strings out of its hide."

It has been Old Op who has spouted the tallest tales as the gospel truth to anyone he let get close enough to him to listen. His storytelling art could be so distracting to his fellow sprout cutters or hoers that he could easily hold the championship for speed among them. Several of his favorites told in *Good Spirit* related to snakes:

> "One night I's out to Six Hickories a-possum huntin' with old Jerry and I carried a blanket with me and laid down on it at about three in the mornin' and looked up at the stars and was a-thinkin' about who all was up in that land beyond the blue and I begin to feel somethin' wiggle under me. I couldn't see too well then. . . . But I jumped up when Jerry got back from a long hunt. I raised up the blanket and old Jerry grabbed somethin' and begin to shake it apart. One of the biggest copperheads ever kilt on Laurel Ridge. Longer than a fence post and big around as my forearm. He was an old residenter that had crawled from the Artner rocks down under."

Op's snake yarns just about convinced fearful Alf Pruitt that quick death in Dayton, Ohio, by atom bombing, was much to be preferred to the slow, painful death by a mountain copperhead bite.

In true folk-tale fashion Op localized his stories:

". . . onct when I was a-walkin' from Honeywell, jist along about where the dump pile is beside the Sandy, Sallie Artner come along there a-drivin' one of Old Fidis' gray hosses hitched to the buggy. . . . I could tell somethin' was the matter. I ran over and held the hoss, put my foot on the buggy stirrup, and went up into that buggy jist in time. Sallie was about to breathe her last. A big cow snake had planted itself in the buggy when it was in the barn entry. . . . It had crawled up under 'er dress 'n' wrapped itself around three 'r four times 'n' was a-squeezin' 'er to death. I tore part of 'er dress off to get to the snake, cut it in two in nine places to get it off. Figured she'd rather be embarrassed than dead. She'd tell you if she's here now, but she lives in Baltimore."

But the biggest one got away:

". . . Right betwixt the spring and where we took a bath I onct laid down across a log to drink from a purty little spring where the water biled up from the ground. I was jist beginnin' to drink when the log started movin'. I guess that was the biggest snake ever seen in these parts. He made a path up the peavine, like where a hoss had pulled a small log. And I followed 'im from behind. I didn't get too close afeared he'd turn and swaller me whole. . . . I've never heard of anybody ever a-killin' that big snake. Boy, there're some gollywhoppin' snakes on Laurel Ridge."

Op seems to have had the same snake in mind when he told of seeing a snake stretched out among the pea vines and wild oats twelve 'or fifteen feet—a snake that he gave a headache by beating it with a heavy pole. In one version the snake "tore down a two-acre field of wheat after he addled it."

Grandpa Tussie in *Taps*, had the boy Sid spellbound with accounts of lumberjack days in the Michigan woods:

> "I drove forty oxen. . . . all in the same team. . . . When I drove my team across a holler with a big tree, I've seen ten yoke of oxen a-hangin' in the air. Cattle would drag 'em right over the bank till they could get their feet down."

And the log the oxen were pulling was so big that "they could run four sets of a square dance on its stump." There would still be room on the stump for the fiddler, banjo picker, and two guitars. "Michigan is some place."

In the same context Grandpa Tussie told a fish story: "The fishes come through a hole in the mountain. . . . Men killed 'em with clubs as they come out. They came through a hole no bigger than a nail keg. Some weighed thirty pounds."

An interesting device of a "fish story" within a fish story occurred in *The Good Spirit of Laurel Ridge,* when Op took city-born Alf bow-and-arrow fishing at Cedar Riffles in the Little Sandy River, a place where the water was shallow enough for wading: "It's a lot better'n trappin' 'em. . . . A man matches his brains with the fish's this way. . . ." They landed a thirty- to forty-pound "red hoss" in the shallow water that night, but Op had caught a much bigger one:

> ". . . He started pullin' and I knew my line would break. But I had my hand down his mouth and behind his gill. I had my feet behind a stump and I pulled with all the power in me and pulled 'im onto the sand. . . . I wrestled with that fish there on the sand till I weakened 'im and hollered to Brother Adger. . . . He found me a-layin'

beside the fish with one hand in his mouth and one arm around him, both of us a-kickin' and a-floppin'. Brother Adger tied him good and tight to a tree with two 'r three strands of trot-line through his gills. . . . He put a fence rail through his gills and carried 'im to Honeywell. His tail drug the ground and he weighed seventy-seven pounds. And when we cleaned 'im we found a sixteen-pound pike inside 'im he'd swallered."

Stuart, willing to admit that the destruction was somewhat exaggerated, insisted upon the basic truth of the owl story, told in "Uncle Casper." A barred hoot owl was caught in a steel trap as a chicken thief, saturated with coal oil (kerosene), set afire, and turned "back to the elements":

"I hollered to Chuck to shoot him with a pistol before he fired the whole country. Chuck put seven balls of lead at that owl. But it soared right on through the elements. It went right over Mart Haley's timber. The blaze shot up like flames from hell. Flames lapped right up through the dead saw briers and leaves. . . . I tell you, gentlemen, that owl set fire to the whole country. My land was ruined. My timber was burned to death. That fire burnt up one thousand panels of rail fence for me. It ruined my meadows. It ruined my neighbors. We had to get together and have workin's and put the fence back. We had to put some barns back and two houses."

Old Op told tall tales about the men he worked with and for (even about Stuart himself). One of these dealt with a spree of Uncle Jake's: ". . . he once got drunk and lay in a four-foot drift of snow. He was so hot he melted the snow for thirty feet around him and a small river ran from Uncle Jake." Another dealt with Minton Artner's butting the ram. A bit of tall-tale exaggeration not associated with Uncle Op was Jason Whiteapple's means of killing a beef—"just *cut drive* with his fist and killed the beef."

Tales of big eaters popular throughout the hills often purport to be the truth, as in Stuart's account of one of his own contemporaries, Mighty Jake who at one time weighed 369 pounds and was "broader than a corncrib across the shoulders":

> I had seen him at one meal drink ten bottles of soft drinks, eat from four to six pounds of steak, ham, turkey, or put away two to three chickens and his share of all the other things on the table. Then for dessert he'd eat a pie, drink a pot of coffee, and smoke a dozen nine-inch cigars. Through the evening he would nibble on a pound box of chocolates.

The tough man about to be hanged in "Sunday Afternoon Hanging" had a like appetite.

The account of a nine-foot sweet potato on display in a Greenup store window is a bit of local lore that pays tribute to the gardening ability of the Daugherty family. This is not in the true tall-tale class of the big turnip (well known in Stuart's region) that burst out the fences on all sides.

One of the best, if not the very best, of Stuart's tall tales is Old Op's account of his ride on the Devil's back on Laurel Ridge one night. First he described the huge, playful Devil in vivid detail:

> "Ye never saw the speret of man with a pair of horns above his ears that come out about two feet from the side of his head and bent back like oxbows, did ye? . . . His skin was somethin' like a bearskin, only the hair was longer. And when I looked at his feet I saw he had the cloven hoof. . . . He had shoulders broader than my cabin door and a big unshaven face somethin' like a bear's. He had a full set of teeth that looked like small white handspikes. He had mule ears he could twitch in the direction of any sound."

Jerry, Op's dog, forsook him for the first time in his life.

> " 'Get on my back, Op,' the Devil said, speakin' plain
> with a voice as big as the roar of waters in April down at
> Sandy Falls. . . . I leaped up on his back like a ground
> squirrel. I took him by the horns and swung my weight
> up to his shoulders. Put a leg over each shoulder and a
> hand on each horn."

At this point Alf Pruitt tried to stop Op, but the old man
was determined to finish the story:

> "Now right along here was where the Devil started
> trottin' with me. . . . He jogged up and down so I
> thought he was a-tryin' to throw me off. . . . Fire streaked
> like lightnin' from his feet. . . . Then suddenly the Devil
> changed his pace. He started rackin'!"

In front of Op's shack, the Devil stopped and let him off,
then disappeared amid thunder and lightning—and Op
went to bed and slept like a log. "If I ever got on his back
agin, I would shore dehorn him," he ended his story.

A blend of folk humor and original humor in the American folk tradition has lightened the darkest pages of Stuart's depiction of his native folk culture. *The Good Spirit of
Laurel Ridge, Taps for Private Tussie,* and *Trees of Heaven*
have been accurately described as folk novels; Stuart's poetry, autobiography, and short stories have been no less rich
than the novels in the folklore and humor of his region. Stuart's humor has reached into every corner of hill life. For
the most part, it has been characterized by tall-tale exaggeration, grotesque naturalism, and homely expression.

Stuart's manner of telling a story has usually combined
monologue and dialogue. He has often taken the viewpoint
of a naïve but observant child, a vantage point for frequent
touches of dramatic irony. The style has been offhand and

unpretentious, full of clichés and repetitions; the stories, often plotless, sometimes have simply raised a question and resolved it with an economy of incident akin to old ballads. "The humorous story is told gravely," Mark Twain once said; "the teller does his best to conceal the fact that he even dimly suspects that there is anything funny about it."

With surface seriousness, Stuart has written of fantastic acts of hill men and hill women with eccentric addictions, of the antics of hill tricksters and their dupes, of the foibles and drolleries of his people. The humor of grotesque metaphor and pithy old proverb has been ubiquitous in his stories. His "serious truthful talk" has sometimes carried an edge of satire. In general, his humor has belonged to the type that uses overstatement in the selection of material and understatement in the manner of presenting it.

Much of the humor has been simple exaggeration. In "Toes," a man with a peg leg was so lazy that the *peckerwoods* drilled a hole in his wooden leg while he slept, and on another occasion he went to sleep close to a brush fire and his peg leg burned almost off before he could find the energy to unstrap it. In "Whose Land Is This?" Uncle Uglybird deplored the decline of his spitting power—"ust to hit a snake's eye at twenty feet."

An unusual, or even grotesque, detail has often provided humor. Georgia Greene prayed loud in church for "seedy sinners," but she liked to chew tobacco and "drink her kerosene." The Barnie mule won a twenty-five-dollar wager for his master when he pulled a hay wagon from the mire— while his owner dangled in front of his nose a *poke* of strong chewing tobacco ("I don't give him but a chaw every mornin'"). A mongrel dog, that had attached itself to a moonshiner, became an alcoholic and was saved only by his master's arrest in *Mongrel Mettle*.

Somewhat more grim has been the grotesquerie of death. In "A Land Beyond the River," the detail recurred that a dying man who had been shot through the heart "pulled up one leg like a frog swimming." In "Bird-Neck" an old man in his eighties sold his body to a hospital for twenty-five dollars, paid his taxes, and bought a jug of whisky with the money; then he cheated the hospital by hanging himself high in a leafy tree ("he wouldn't die off'n his land if he could help it"). In "The Word and the Flesh" the survivors of the copperhead bites were a grotesque lot: one had a fleshless leg bone; one a hole in his jaw through which the food squirmed when he ate; a man in one field plowed with his right arm, and one in a neighboring field had only his left arm to use. In "The Ballad of Lonesome Waters" a false true-love returned to his sweetheart after she had borne five daughters to One-eyed Jim; Jim's gun forced Dave to give Liddie Bee one-armed hugs and made the plowing rather hard, but "then it did not do his body harm."

Deception has been prominent in Stuart's humor. In "Hair" a ribald touch suggestive of medieval fabliau entered into the rejected suitor's seduction of the girl he had always loved. Adger Akers rationalized in court that he had impersonated God at Six Hickories Church not with the idea of disturbing public worship but to see whether the people "really did want the Lord, Our Saviour, to visit 'em or not." Judd Sluss made no such rationalization of his appearing as God to Old Peter Leadingham. Humorous deceptive bargains took place in "Hot-Collared Mule" and "The Chase of the Skittish Heifer."

When Stuart has used satire, it has usually been directed against beliefs and practices that have interfered with education, sound morality, security, and the simple enjoyment of family and community life. Judge Allie in *Foretaste of Glory* was "a religious man who didn't cuss, smoke, or drink"—but who rejected his illegitimate son. An incident illustrating the evils of the trustee system in *The Thread That Runs So True* gave an account of rivalry amounting to feuding between two churches for control of a tiny hill school—with little attention to the school facilities. In *Foretaste of Glory* most of the repentant sinners had waited until they thought they were facing Doomsday.

More often than satire, irony has been Stuart's vehicle for humor. In "Battle with the Bees" a bee stealer became the victim of his own bees, which had been the bane of his family's existence. In "The Wind Blew East" a woman noted for her perfect houskeeping was driven from her home by skunk scent in her attic. Isser Pennington had no recourse when the hair tonic "guaranteed to grow hair on a fish" grew none on Isser's head—"The hair tonic showed he wasn't a fish."

The folklore and humor in Stuart's works have shown the strong influence of an earlier and more homogeneous folk tradition, with a predominance of Anglo-American elements. As Gordon Wilson has remarked of his native western Kentucky community, much of the W-Hollow and Greenup County lore is now taken only half-seriously and some of it even comically. That this material and Stuart's treatment of it have modern appeal has been demonstrated by the wide range of his publishing media: high-school textbooks, children's books, women's magazines, men's magazines, university reviews, educational journals, religious and trade publications, as well as popular magazines and books. His work in its totality preserves the folklore and folk customs of three generations in the W-Hollow region of northeastern Kentucky.

CHAPTER TWO

The Hill Man's Religion

But the hill people still saw God. . . .

BEYOND DARK HILLS

With less of social protest than of humor, Jesse Stuart has brought alive the *old-time religion* with its narrow intolerance, its dark superstition, and at the same time its undeniable sustaining power. The strange blend of self-contradictory elements that made up hill church doctrine was as basic in hill thinking as were the religious gatherings in the social life and in the personal relationships of the people. Stuart's vivid descriptions of the highly emotional scenes of *a hill revival, a spring baptizing, a footwashing,* an *Association,* a *funeralizing,* and other religious meetings have communicated the hill man's concepts of Heaven, Hell, God, the Devil, sin, and *living by the Word,* with each detail concretely envisioned. Here, as in other phases of hill life, Stuart's use of folk speech has provided the outsider with a key to help him understand the concepts, attitudes, and conduct of the of hill people.

The Good Book, the Holy Bible, was often the only book a hill family owned, and the reverence that even illiterate people felt for it was closely akin to magic. Stuart recalled of his early childhood: "We had only one book in our shack.

That was the Bible." The *Word* could refer to the Bible, to God, or to a *call to preach* (*got the Word*). The Bible was the one book which the hill people considered worth reading; and they were thoroughly convinced—many of them —that its meaning would be divinely revealed to true believers: "Don't have to go to school. . . . Just have the faith and open the Word and read." The preachers in Stuart's stories, like their real life counterparts, have consequently quoted and misquoted the Bible in support of farfetched notions of right and wrong and to explain very peculiar conduct. When a hill man said, "Don't it say in the Word," he was not asking a question but making a confident assertion, no matter how bizarre his thinking may have seemed to an outsider. The Word, based on the Scriptures or distorted from the Bible passages, was the key expression to hill religion.

When the Tussies gained the prosperity of Kim's $10,000 government insurance, Grandma made a remark that illustrated a typically grotesque application of Biblical language to everyday living and the hill tendency to interweave religion and folklore: "Money's like *manna* from heaven. . . . I've always dreamed of finding a pot of gold where a shootin' star fell. . . . This is the pot of gold I've always looked for!" Grandma could foresee that the Tussies' riches would bring relatives down upon them *like locusts in their seasons to eat up the trees.* Uncle George Tussie, one of the *locusts,* was sure that he had Scriptural basis for thinking that Vittie, Kim's widow, would get her reward in Heaven for the way she was using her dead husband's insurance money: "I was given plenty to eat, a good bed to sleep in, and today *you clothed me.* Ain't there something in the Word about clothin' a man?" When the owner of the big Rayburn house gave the eviction notice, Grandpa Tussie was even more certain that he had Biblical support for his advice to the forty-six Tussies who had come to live with him: "That's what the Word tells us. *Dance and be merry for tomorrow you may die.*" He accepted the supposed death of his son and the loss of his old-age pension with fortitude: *Man born of woman is full of trouble;* and *every man must have his Judas.* Grandma distorted the Biblical proverb only a little in reference to Vittie's marriage to Uncle George: *Give 'em the wind. That is what they've sown, and the wind's what they'll reap.* Not for the primitive Tussies, but in reference to his own energetic family was Stuart's mention of the ancient fable of the ant and the grasshopper: *Go, thou sluggard, like the ant and be wise.*

The lusting of the flesh led some hill men to *know* a woman before marriage, but most of them felt that once they had married they should not *put asunder what God had jined together.* When a logger killed his rival logger for committing adultery with his wife, the murderer went free in court; but the relatives of the dead man pointed out the sign on the courthouse: *God is not mocked. Whatsoever a man soweth that shall he also reap.* They were threatening him with the stern mountain code that called for *an eye for an eye, a man for a man.* Ronnie, who had "two livin' wives right down there together" was *a-livin' in adult'ry,* for which he was much at fault *in the eyes of the Lord.* When Brother Fain Groan tried to show his faith in the Word by resurrecting his dead wife, even his *Disciples* felt doubtful about carrying husbandly affection so far: "It is against the *Word* to *prank* with the dead. Don't the Word say, 'Let the dead rest. Bury the dead and let them rest'?" Phoeby's husband Dave took a more usual attitude when he submitted stoically and said over her coffin, with characteristic mountain fatalism, *Thy will be done.*

Unexpected associations of Biblical terminology with details of hill life have sometimes shown evidence of the hill man's straight-faced humor, but even then have indicated the far-reaching influences of the Bible on hill speech and thought: a reference to Kentucky hill Republicans as the *Lost Tribe of Israel,* a revenue officer's badge as the *Mark o' the Beast,* a clever trader as a *wolf in sheep's clothing.* Less intentional on the part of the illiterate hill preacher than on the part of Jesse Stuart was the humor of a somewhat jumbled funeral tribute to soldier Kim Tussie: "Like *David* of old, who *slew the Philistines with the jawbone of an ass,* Kim *barked* our enemies with his rifle. I know that Kim has entered the *pearly gates* of Heaven!" The context was hardly that of the original when Arn Sparks consoled her son whose hound dog had been poisoned, *Don't let your heart be troubled.* Old Op, annoyed at his city visitor's disbelief in ghosts, asked him indignantly, "Don't the speret leave the body atter we wear out these old clay temples of ourn? . . . Don't ye believe in the *Good Book?*" More literally perhaps than Enoch of old, the Stuart children, on their way to school and Sunday school, *walked with God—* "What did we care about the bull in Wheeler's pasture?"

The love of nature has prompted Stuart's repeated use of the Bible verse, *the Heavens declare the glory of God.* In various contexts he has also repeatedly referred to man's *bringing forth fruit in his season,* and to Bible terms associated with death: when a person had lived his *threescore years and ten* (often Stuart refers to his *fourscore years and ten*) and *had neared the end of his travail upon God's footstool,* he *confessed his sins before men* and hoped to find his name written in the *Lamb's Book of Life.* All except the most *wicked* hill men looked forward to taking their places before the *Throne of God* where *God would wipe away all tears,* and there would be no hunger or thirst or any other troubles that had beset the person on earth. The book of Revelation has had a particular fascination for the hill people, and their interpretations have been fearfully and wonderfully concrete and literal. Yet never has this apocalyptic vision affected their trust in God's personal and benevolent concern for them, as expressed in Uncle John the Baptist's ringing song, *His eye is on the sparrow, and I know he watches me.* Judge Allie Anderson's illegitimate son, Rufus Litteral, unclaimed until the supposed *day of doom,* also found great comfort in the Scriptures.

When a hill preacher *got the Word,* his belief that God had divinely called and inspired him to lead others in the paths of righteousness, most of the members of his congregations shared the attitude of the child Jesse Stuart, "I thought all the preacher said just had to be true." Some of them *got the Word* very suddenly, as did Brother Melvin P. Hankas. He *got under conviction* at one of Brother Peter Leadingham's revivals: ". . . the next day I was on a mowin' machine and I felt like I had a sunstroke. Right there me and my Lord got right, and He put his hand on my head and said, 'Preach.' I went to preachin' in three days." The real-life incident that inspired this story was a reiterated story in Brother Tobbie's sermons at Plum Grove. Stuart's mother told him during one of his college vacations: "Yes, he [Brother Tobbie] did go over that old story again about the Lord calling him to preach when he was a-cuttin' hay on that piece of ground back of the barn." An unlooked-for answer to a skeptic's prayer launched another hill man into the ministry. Silas Woodberry, amazed into conversion by the storm that washed out his milldam, prayed that God would help him to catch the *drifting souls* and give him the *heaviest cross to bear.* Hank Redfern also *got the Word* suddenly and began to preach. When the Reverend Adam Flint was preaching the funeral of a man who resembled Stuart's maternal grandfather, he spoke of boyhood visions in the cornfield and how he could suddenly read the Word, preach, and *line out* hymns from the *Old Sweet Songster.*

The illiteracy of the preachers and a widespread tendency to argue over doctrine and take pride in considering one's own interpretations direct messages from God himself led to unreasoning intolerance among denominations and to divisiveness within denominations. In "The Anglo-Saxons of Auxierville" Stuart was being more truthful than facetious when he wrote: "Their spirits will leave their temples of clay for one of the eight Baptist Heavens." Revivals with their supercharge of emotionalism did much to encourage the dogmatic attitude that the hill people took toward their chosen churches, each believing that only his church had the *right kind of Faith* and a *promise of the Glory Land.* Although Methodist, Holy Roller, Unknown Tongue, and certin other sects have found a place in Stuart's writings, as they have in hill religious life, his stories have reflected the overwhelming predominance of the Baptist doctrine in the region. His comic muse has been much in evidence in stories picturing the difficulties that Mountain Baptists have had in agreeing, or disagreeing, among themselves.

In "Love in the Spring" Elster's fourth-generation Methodist parents threatened to disown him if he yielded to his love in the spring and married that *infidel,* the *Slab Baptis'* girl Effie; but it was a knockout blow from her *Slab Baptis'* boyfriend following his declaration that he "ain't no damned *infidental*" that sent Elster back home and into the Methodist fold. In "Weep No More My Lady" it was only because of her misunderstanding that the Mountain Baptist widow married a Free Will Baptist as her second husband. In "Three Hundred Acres of Elbow Room" Big Eif Porter insisted upon his son's *norrating* among his neighbors— especially the *Free Willers*—the news of his *token* that he was to *change worlds* that night at ten o'clock and urged them to be present so that they would know that the *Forty-Gallon Baptists* (the name Stuart has given one of the divisions of Mountain Baptists who approved of drinking mountain whisky) had the *right kind of faith* and the *true religion.* "Uncle John the Baptist" in the story of that title was just as thoroughly convinced that the *Free Willers* had the inside track to Heaven. Uncle Mel Shelton, who was considered by many to be an *infidel* standing in the way of many with his *set idears on the Bible,* inspired his nephew to have a vision of the afterlife:

> If you could see all of us Republicans, Democrats, Methodists, Forty-Gallon Baptists, Hard-shelled Baptists, Free-will Baptists, Primitive Baptists, Regular Baptists, United Baptists, Missionary Baptists, Union Baptists, Independent Baptists—all of us out'n the graves a-shaking hands and asking the other how he is after the long night o' sleep . . . how great it all is. . . .

When Baptist and Methodist preachers stopped preaching *holiness* and the *coming of the millennium* and discouraged shouting and other such displays, some of the oldtimers became uncomfortable and formed new sects, each stubbornly holding that its members were *the only people right.* Stuart has coined and often used as a blanket term for these sects that split off from the Baptist and Methodist churches the name the *Church of the Old-Fashioned Faith.* The rapid growth of such sects as the Church of God, Pilgrim Holiness, Church of the Nazarene, Pentecostal, and others during the depression years of the 1930s when Stuart was publishing his first books and stories unquestionably influenced his writings.

Stuart's portrayal of hill preachers has often leaned toward the extremes of corruptness and fanaticism, and he has been inclined to deal with the uniquely grotesque incidents rather than the typical; but he has also shown insight in his occasional incidents dealing with hill preachers who were sincere men of integrity and sympathetic concern for the hill people. In the former category were such men as the preacher the boy Jesse Stuart saw with a woman in the weeds by the creek bank. "He gave me twenty-five cents and . . . told me not to say anything about seeing him there." Brother Hammertight collected *sinful* jewelry from repentant sinners and sold it across the river in West Virginia, following the practice of corrupt churchmen since pre-Reformation days. Brother Tobbie, who committed suicide by putting a double-barreled shotgun to his temple, *wasn't nigh right with the Lord;* Brother Fain Groan, who said of the ten virgins parable, "You know there was ten of them, don't you? And you know one of them was Virgin Mary, don't you?" was not typical in his ignorance nor in his fanatical faith—nor was he alone! It would not be difficult, however, in the 1960s to find preachers still haranguing against television, swimming, and women's clothing; people believing that a person who does not show emotion and shout and testify during a church service has not been *born again.*

Brother Osborne represented the better type of hill preacher:

> He is the shepherd to the flock of hill people in Greenup Country. He preaches to them. He marries them. He preaches their funerals. He comes to their bed in time of sickness. He rides on horseback or walks. He goes to them in their time of need.

At the funeral of Mrs. Waters, the insane suicide, his words were gentle and compassionate—unlike the preaching of so many old-time preachers—full of God's love for his struggling people.

When the preachers' faults were born of ignorance and naïveté rather than of greed, lust, and deceit, Stuart has portrayed them as pathetic rather than evil. For example, the young girl snake-handler of the *Unknown Tongue* church was presented with almost idyllic sweetness in "Snake Teeth." Humor took the reins in "Red Jacket: The Knockin' Sperit," when Old Brother Peter Leadingham fell prey to prankster Judd Sluss. Brother Peter boasted: "God is just a common man. . . . God is about the size of Judd Sluss. . . . God smokes a pipe just like I do and the same brand of tobacco. . . . I'm the only skunk livin' that has seen his Saviour face to face."

In the Kentucky hills, unlike some of the highland communities, very few immigrant Catholics were attracted by the development of public works, and the preachers and members of their congregations alike were militantly Protestant. Stuart reflected this antipathy toward Roman Catholics in his account of a hitchhiking incident. The Catholic truck driver with whom he had ridden the night before had been invited along with Stuart to eat breakfast in a Kentucky mountain home, and the farmer's wife had offered him ham and gravy. " 'No, madam. I don't eat meat on Friday. It is against my religion. I am a Catholic.' Mrs. Tillman acted like she had been hit above the eye." In the course of the conversation Mr. Tillman felt impelled to knock the man down from the table. The next person to give Stuart a ride, upon hearing of the incident, expressed just as strong anti-Catholic feeling, saying meaningfully, "I'm a Klansman."

Most of the hill preachers and members of their congregations had a dual concept of God as a fearful physical presence and as a benevolent protector. The young Jesse Stuart thought of God as ready to "jump from behind a tree and hit me with a stick."

> . . . Everybody there had the same picture of God. He was a strong man that rode the clouds. He saw through a tree. He took the good people home and sent the bad people to the Devil. God and the Devil were at war. They had many fights there at Plum Grove.

Granny Flaugherty's dream of Heaven with its harp-playing angels and a fatherly God on his *Great Throne* is one of many Stuart pictures of God's benevolence. The details of this vision were impressed upon the young Stuart by Granny's much-repeated account of her visit there. Relatives, neighbors, and friends who had *gone to Glory* met her there with as warm a welcome as if she had been paying a neighborly visit in Kentucky. It seemed a most democratic place in which God smiled upon his *sanctified* followers. When *the good old Soul* died at ninety-three her neighbors felt sure she had become *one of God's angels*. Sister Combs of the Unknown Tongue faith preached in a hill revival: "What will you do in Heaven for whisky and terbacker? There will be no saloons there. There will be no spittoons there. You will not want to dirty the *streets of gold* with old black *ambeer* spit. You will not want to get drunk in Heaven." Young Sid, listening to the funeral sermon for his uncle Kim in *Taps for Private Tussie*, wonders about Brother Baggs' picture of Heaven: "I don't think that Heaven with golden streets and good people would suit Uncle Kim," rough, profane, hard-drinking, pistol-shooting mountain man that he had been on earth.

Big Eif Porter deviated a little further from the Scriptures when he hoped that Heaven would provide him with a "farm where I can work, and I hope they have winter, summer, springtime, and fall there just like we have here." He thought of death as "somethin' like a-goin' from my farm over to Wormwood's farm," and he hoped that his neighbors would "live on adjoining farms" in Heaven. He thought it might take "a hour to get up that long ladder a body's got to go up before he gets to Heaven." Old Peter Leadingham also thought of Heaven as quite near—just a mile or two above his head. The title *Plowshare in Heaven* (1958) suggests this tendency toward concreteness in religious concepts as a basic element in hill religion. As in certain traditional folk ballads, characters were unable—or unwilling—to distinguish between the flesh and the spirit. Phoeby in the title story "Plowshare in Heaven" saved money to buy a new dress, "the dress I want to wear in Heaven. . . ." Shan, the small boy in this story, doubted that Phoeby would be happy in Heaven as the Bible has described it.

> "It will not be home unless she can walk barefooted over the fields of growing corn and feel the soft earth beneath her feet; unless she can feel the handle of a hoe in her hand and smell the good clean wind of a Kentucky spring. . . ."

The funeral songs of the mountain people, as Stuart has recorded them, have shown the deep need of hard-working men and women to think of Heaven as a place of eternal rest: "The Land Beyond the River," "Rock of Ages," "Leaning on the Everlasting Arms," and "Where the Living Waters Flow":

> There is a land of wondrous beauty
> Where the "Living Waters" flow,
> The word of God to all has said it
> And it surely must be so.
>
> No tears are there, no blighting sorrow
> From the cruel hand of Death;
> No flowers fade, no summers perish
> By the winter's chilling breath.
>
> I've loved ones there who passed before me,
> They'll rejoice to see me come,
> But best of all, I'll see my Saviour,
> Who will bid me welcome home.

Other favorites have been "Amazing Grace," "From Greenland's Icy Mountains," "When Winter's Darkling Waves We'll Ferry O'er," "We'll Meet You in the Morning Over There," "Safe in the Arms of Jesus," and "The Sweet Bye and Bye."

The mountain man's visualizing of Hell and the Devil has been equally vivid. Anse Bushman, during his period of unconsciousness after a tree had fallen on him, saw himself in the *lake of fire and brimstone* trying to swim amid serpents and scorpions that wore the heads of his sinful earthly neighbors. Old Peter Leadingham's concept, however phony his vision in the beech grove, was of a fierce Devil carrying a pitchfork in his hand: "He has the horns of a two-year-old bull and he looks somethin' like a black cow walkin' on her hind feet." Old Op, too, had a tall-tale experience with the Devil. These stories, partaking of practical joking and folk tale, are extreme; but the picture of a physical devil in the image of man—but with horns, tail, and cloven hoof—was as widely held among the hill people of the past as was the anthropomorphic concept of God.

Literal, too, was the hill man's belief that the body would be resurrected in physical form on the *Judgment Day*. Uncle Mel Shelton in "This Is the Place" spoke for many:

> "We shall be as we have been—have the same color of hair, shapes of noses, the same voice—We shall run with our old company—I expect to have my farm here and do the things as I have always done. How can that which is the real Mel Shelton die? . . . It was not born to die—only the husk that encloses it was born to die."

The belief in *Christ's Second Coming* in the clouds followed by the *millennium,* or thousand years of peace, that had been revived by European pietists from the beliefs of the early Christians has been the subject of much discussion among the highland population, particularly in time of war or the threat of war. It has lost ground in recent years, but only two decades ago events that took place one night in Blakesburg (Greenup) demonstrated conclusively that the concept of the *Judgment Day* was almost universal among the townspeople there as well as among the Red Necks, or country people.

An unusually brilliant showing of the aurora borealis on September 18 was mistaken for *the end of the world, the end of time, the Judgment Day, Christ's coming on a cloud.* This naïve interpretation of a natural phenomenon uncommon so far south inspired a whole gallery of portraits of frightened men and women in Stuart's *Foretaste of Glory.* People so visual-minded, whose very lives depended often on elemental nature, found it easy to explain natural phenomena and uneasy states of mind in terms of the supernatural. Some—not all—hill preachers and *exhorters* exploited this tendency to the full. The Reverend Mr. Whetstone, retired minister, could not get an audience when he tried to quiet the people with the scientific explanation. Sister Spence, assisted by *exhorter* Bert Edgwater in the courthouse square, pleaded: "This will be your last time to repent! Oh, why not be saved before it is too late! A home in Glory and the promise of eternal life is better than a-goin' to a Devil's hell to spend your eternity in fire and brimstone! . . ." As his fellow townsmen rushed about taking advantage of what they thought was a last chance to *get right* with God and man, the gravedigger Uncle Uglybird Skinner and Judge Allie Anderson down at his hogpen remarked uncertainly: *The end of time comes in a twinkling. . . . Not even the angels in Heaven will know when it comes.* The majority of characters in *Foretaste of Glory,* however, brought to the surface their innermost, and often guilty, secrets as they looked fearfully upon the signs in the skies; until they had fully confessed their sins, they felt unprepared *to meet their Maker* on the *Day of Doom.*

Mountain religion is full of contradictions. Kentucky historian Thomas D. Clarke has written in *A History of Kentucky* of the early pioneers as applying "a practical religious belief of foreordination to their daily lives." The passage continues:

> . . . Nearly everyone believed that his fate was a sealed book and very philosophically accepted his hardships as God-sent. This belief is typical of people who live close to nature. Religion on the frontier was as rugged and hard as the virgin oak. . . (pp. 106–107).

Even within his own family Stuart has recognized this fatalistic element in hill belief. But this does not in the least rule out an equally strong belief that each individual participated in his own salvation.

The Calvinistic, Puritan identification of hard work with the good life is a recurrent theme in Stuart's writings and an integral trait of mountain character. Grandpa in the story "Grandpa" states a widely held moral code and religious viewpoint in the following passage of conversation:

> ". . . I am the last leaf. I'm waitin' fer the Master's call. He will call me, too, when he wants me. I'll hear His call. I'll heed that call, fer I am ready. I've cheated no man. I've given away in my lifetime. I have come to the end without land or money. I've wronged no woman, killed no man, stole no chickens, I've cut as many saw logs and cleaned as much of briers and sprouts and trees as any man in Kentucky."

This feeling of a direct, personal relationship between God and man appears everywhere in Jesse Stuart's stories and autobiographies, and is attributed to many types of mountain men and women.

The Word, then, sometimes means the Bible and the good life based on the hill man's understanding or misunderstanding of the Bible; or it may be an illiterate hill preacher's prohibitions of wearing jewelry, using tobacco, dancing, or watching television. *Living by the Word* involves plenty of hard work, occasional *wrestlings with the Devil, owing no man anything,* and accepting whatever comes as *the will of God,* who put everyone and everything here *for a purpose.* Incredibly naïve at times, mountain religion is an intensely personal experience, inseparable from folk custom and the practical details of everyday living; and each sect is sure that its followers alone have *the right kind of faith.*

Almost everyone in the hills, no matter how *wicked (weaked),* intended someday to *get right with God.* In Stuart's accounts of mountain religious conversions humor, sympathetic insight, and critical comment are blended. He has focused attention especially on the spring revivals, which were often rightly called *protracted meetings,* for they sometimes lasted four and five weeks instead of the originally planned two weeks. Some church members backslid repeatedly during the long pent-up winters or during the hard summer work in *crop time,* and had to *get right in their hearts* year after year.

Conversion was due from the time one's *accountability* began at the age of twelve, but in some Stuart stories the lusty old figures of earth had passed their fourscore years and ten before they could bring themselves to give up *worldly things.* Battle Keaton, for example, was past eighty when he *got saved* and *come across on the Lord's side* at a protracted meeting in the schoolhouse on Hog Branch.

Getting saved followed a rather definite pattern, which might extend over hours, days, weeks, or even longer. As soon as the sinner *got under conviction* and went up to kneel at the *mourners' bench,* he began to *wrestle with the devil* in prayer. The praying continued until the *burden was rolled away* and he could bring himself to *confess his sins before men.* Usually his confession was followed by a trance-like state of exaltation proving to him and to all present that God had forgiven his sins. He was then ready to *follow his*

Lord in baptism by immersion in the waters of Little Sandy at Put-Off Ford, and live *on Jesus' side* (*on the Lord's side*). Unless a person had committed the blackest sins or unless he himself felt impatience, the baptism was usually delayed until the big *spring baptizing;* but Stuart's parents' experience of being baptized in weather so cold that a hole had to be chopped in the ice was by no means unique. Only the fortunate few among the converts were righteous enough to achieve *Second Blessing* and *Sanctification* that made it impossible for them to sin thereafter.

The typical hill revival service was noisy and emotional, often with several preachers participating. Although it was the exception rather than the rule for preachers to wear long, flowing white robes, some of the young girl evangelists and a few of the more fanatical men preachers imitated the robes in the Sunday-school card pictures of Christ performing His earthly ministry. The *meetings* often took place in schoolhouses or church houses; but the largest and most exciting ones were held in the groves with the congregation sitting on split-log benches and lanterns hanging from the trees.

The loud harmonized hymn singing, sweet to mountain ears, sounded across the countryside, sometimes to organ or guitar accompaniment, sometimes *lined out* by a leader in churches that ruled out musical instruments and even tuning forks—but nevertheless loved to sing. The revival songs were widely diversified, including many of the old hymns familiar to Evangelical Protestants in the highlands and throughout the South, less familiar old-fashioned selections from the *Old Sweet Songster* and others of its type, and newer songs showing the influence of outland slang and jazz. The style of singing showed the influence of old-style ballad singing in the little grace notes and sharp intake of breath at the end of a phrase, and also the influence of the loud and lusty harmonies of the camp meeting. Stuart has

included texts—and has mentioned many additional songs
—in all three categories.

Note the contrast in tone between "Tho' Coming Weak
and Vile" and "I Would Not Be Denied."

> Tho' coming weak and vile
> Thou dost my strength assure;
> Thou dost my vileness fully cleanse
> So spotless all and pure.
>
> 'Tis Jesus calls me on
> To perfect faith and love,
> To perfect hope, and peace, and trust
> For earth and Heaven above.
>
> And He assurance gives
> To loyal hearts and true,
> That every promise is fulfilled
> To those who bear and do.

The second was popular with the Holiness and Unknown
Tongue churches:

> You can't go to Heaven with powder and paint,
> I would not be denied;
> You'll not catch sight of the golden gate,
> I would not be denied.
>
> The Devil wears a Hypocrite shoe,
> I would not be denied;
> If you don't watch out, he will step on you,
> I would not be denied.

And it continues through many stanzas. Similar to "I Would
Not Be Denied," in tune and tone, is "I've Been Redeemed,"
from which the following are characteristic stanzas:

> You can't go to Heaven on roller skates,
> You'll roll right through Heaven's pearly gates.

I've been redeemed
By the Blood of the Lamb,
Saved and sanctified I am
I've been redeemed. . . .

You can't go to Heaven, girls, and wear a rat,
You can't go to Heaven, men, and carry a gat, etc.

Sometimes surprising elements and influences appeared in these hill church songs, for example, Nancy Cochrane's solo at the Faith Healing Holiness Church in Lonesome Valley, "I'm Naturalized for Heaven."

After the spirited song service, several hours of preaching, exhorting, and praying were accompanied by shouting on the part of anyone in the congregation that the spirit moved to shout (no one, least of all the preacher, considered the *Amens* and *Glory hallelujahs* to be interruptions). The typical sermons concentrated on contrasting the horrors of Hell with the beauties of Heaven, with the former receiving by far the greater emphasis. *Burning forever in the lake of fire and brimstone* was pictured as the awful consequence of such *mortal sins* as the following: raising or smoking the *filthy and evil weed* tobacco—less frequently of drinking whisky; playing cards, going to cockfights, and otherwise gambling; stealing, even so much as a chicken; committing adultery; dancing to fiddle music, or playing it; wearing cosmetics and jewelry; attending movies, baseball games, and carnivals; women's wearing bathing suits, shorts, low-necked and sleeveless dresses; and, more recently, watching television.

When a repentant hill tobacco farmer went home from the revival service and cut his green tobacco by moonlight, some of his fellow church members were worldly enough to wonder how he would feed and clothe his family without the money from his crop. Some sons of pipe-smoking mountain women doubted Brother Toady Leadingham's preach-

ing that a person had to change the color of his spit before
he could go to Heaven, and accused the preacher of getting
off'n the Gospel. One fiery old hill preacher kept a *Scandal
Board* where he mounted the sinful objects—pipes, plugs of
tobacco, rings, guns, knives, steel knucks, and even ten-
dollar bills. Since mountain preachers and their listeners
usually felt that it was wrong for them to take money for
their preaching, the temptation was great to take the sinful
objects across a state line and sell them. Brother Doubty,
who preached just as vociferously against those evils, was
greatly admired for his integrity in refusing all money.
Whether or not they gave up their *pleasures,* the hill men
usually agreed with the preacher that the foregoing things
were *sinful.*

Whatever the subject of his harangue, the preacher accompanied his shouted sermon with a good deal of near-
acrobatic action, although Brother Hammertight may have
carried it to a greater extreme than was usual:

> Brother Hammertight is trying to climb the stovepipe.
> . . . He tears the whole works down. . . . He shouts on.
> . . . "There's the work of the Devil. See that terbacker up
> there. The old Devil has went out of this room by now.
> . . . We've got him on the run. Shout on, Brother, Amen,
> Sister. Shout on. Glory be to God."

Women breast-fed their babies to stop them from crying.
Drunken, pistol-toting young men *carvarted* about and
mocked at the choir as they parodied their song, "I would
not be pop-eyed."

When the sinners began to squirm and feel the presence
of the Devil right at their shoulders, it was time to give the
invitation, which was the climax of every revival service.
Stuart's accounts of the religious hysteria at Plum Grove
and in the outdoor tabernacles of the *Unknown Tongues* are
hardly less extreme than historical accounts of the Cane

Ridge revivals of 1801. Stuart captured the spirit of a hill revival in *Beyond Dark Hills:*

> "There is great rejoicing in Heaven tonight. A sinner here at Plum Grove has repented. . . . Sing the last stanza of 'Nearer, My God, to Thee!' O won't you come? The Lord and the Devil are waiting to see how this meeting is a-comin' out. That's right, sister. Come right up. Now don't be afraid. Others want to, but the Devil won't let them. The Lord is knocking at all their hearts. O won't you come? Praise the Lord they are coming. The Devil is going. . . ."

The saved people tried by song and entreaty to get the sinners down front to the *mourners' bench,* reminding them that *tomorrow's sun may never rise,* this could be their last chance to accept God's promise of *a home in Glory* and *everlasting life.* And the choir sang *Almost persuaded—but lost!* The sinners writhed under their *jolt-wagon loads of sin* until they *prayed through.* The confession of a newly saved soul sometimes caused a less repentant sinner to leave the congregation, especially if he had been an accomplice in adultery. In one story Stuart tells of an *exhorter* of the old logging days who *packed the sinners*—even big lumberjacks, colliers, and ore diggers—down the aisle on his shoulder if they were too slow in going of their own accord. According to Old Op, their confessions were worth hearing. Sometimes the church bell rang out across the fields and hills in the early-morning hours to let the people know that the sinners had all *pulled through.*

The day after a revival or an especially successful Sunday-night service, the conversions would be the talk of the neighborhood:

> "Well, Mrs. Fort came through last night. . . . She finally told the Lord what was the matter with her. She told him she had killed a lot of young babies. . . . When

she said these words she began shouting." "I want to tell you Sy Mullins got religion last night. He's been trying for years. But he could never get right with the Lord. He told all he'd ever done last night. Since Hilder Kameen's wife died he confessed being with her down in the cornfield one time. He would never confess when she was living. . . ."

The big *Spring Baptizing* was a social event that drew people from a radius of five and six miles around. Converts who could afford to buy new clothes bought white dresses if they were young girls, flashy pants, silk shirts, and loud neckties if they were young men. The preacher and two strong men went out to measure the depth of the water with a light fence rail until they found a place free from snags and rocks where the water was the right depth. Meanwhile, the people made their wagons and buggies secure or hitched their mules and horses where they would not be in danger of sliding into the water.

The same baptizing seems to have inspired the detailed descriptions in *Beyond Dark Hills* and in "Braska Comes Through." When each person being baptized went down into the water, the choir sang "Shall We Gather at the River," and after he had been immersed the people sang "Where the Healing Waters Flow."

> Sister Tister is the first to follow the preacher into the brown swirling water. It gathers up her clothes tight around her legs and body. When the water is close under her arms, they stand. He waves his hand for the choir on the bank to sing:
>
> > Yes, we shall gather at the river.
> > There the saints of our fathers trod,
> > Yes, we shall gather at the river,
> > The beautiful, the beautiful river
> > That flows by the throne of God.

> There is a splash of water. Words have been said. Sister
> Tister is up and she is shouting. The two strong men keep
> her from running into the deep water or from hitting a
> snag. Women on the river bank are sobbing and shouting.
> She comes out of the river shouting. She shouts all over
> the bank. She goes down exhausted. She begins to jerk, ly-
> ing stretched out in her wet clothes on the sand.

Some of the wet men and women went into the bushes to
change their clothing, but others wore their clinging gar-
ments home, as the more modest way. Until the following
year, there would not be another such *baptizing*.

Not all mountain churches practiced *footwashing*, not
even all Mountain Baptist churches; but among those who
practiced it, the ceremonial was significant and private.
Stuart has given a detailed description of a *footwashing* in
the short story "Love in the Spring," which he localized as
taking place at Put-Off Ford in Little Sandy, scene of many
baptizings. The Slab Baptists looked upon visitors from
other denominations as the *Devil in sheep's clothing*, and
did not hesitate to let the Plum Grove Methodist boy know
that he was not welcome. *Bitten by the love bug right
above the heart* when he saw Effie, the Slab Baptist girl, he
stayed and watched:

> . . . A whole row up and a whole row down. The row
> standing up was a-washing the feet of them on the
> ground. Just setting there on the ground as unconcerned
> and washing feet. Then they would sing another verse of
> "Where the Healing Waters Flow."
>
> . . . .
>
> . . . Some man had his back to me. He was washing her
> foot. He had an old chipped washpan and a big towel
> and a bar of home-made soap made from oak-tree ashes.
> He'd put it on her foot till it would look pink as a wild
> crab-apple blossom.

Effie's Slab Baptist sweetheart glared at Elster: "Go on about your business . . . and leave us Baptis alone. This ain't no side show. We are here worshiping the Lord."

Uncle Uglybird in one of his stories of an earlier day at Six Hickories Church on Laurel Ridge referred to the big *protracted meetings* and the *footwashings*. In response to a question as to where the people got water to wash one another's feet, he replied:

> "Took lanterns and pine torches and went down to that sulphur spring under the hill in the beech grove. . . . There was a path worn over the hill to that spring in them days slick as the path to a groundhog hole."

As at so many of the hill gatherings, fights were not unusual at the footwashings. Stuart also has made other references to them, but the details seem to have been less familiar to him than those of the revival meetings and baptizings. In "A Yard of String" the narrator told of breaking his little finger in two places when he *hit a fellow at a footwashing*.

The Baptist *Association* held annually throughout the denomination had a particular social significance in the hill communities. Baptists from one or more counties met to report on the year's work and make plans for the coming year; they *fellowshiped* together, listened to budget reports and long sermons, ate much fried chicken, and gloried in being Baptists. In *Trees of Heaven* the mountain woman Fronnie told her neighbors at the *molasses-making* about attending the Big Baptist Association at Mountain Chapel —"about this Baptist preacher and that Baptist preacher and how long each preached and she can tell a few things that each said in his two-, three-, and four-hour sermons."

Probably the same event gave rise to the story "Uncle John, the Baptist," describing a *Free Willer Baptist Association* that lasted three days at Mountain Chapel, while much trading went on nearby: "Just can't trade within two hundred yards of the preacher," Uncle John explained. The description of the scene at Mountain Chapel suggested similar meetings throughout the Southern mountains:

> . . . We walk across the tradin' grounds to the head of a little stream. . . . People are sittin' under the trees on rocks, on the ground, on half-split logs. Down below them is a big platform built . . . five logs high and covered with a puncheon floor. Across this are logs split in two and held up by huge blocks of round trees. Men with long beards are settin' on these seats sayin' "Amen" to the "Word" Brother High is preachin'.
> "Amen," says Uncle John, walkin' up to the platform. "Praise the Lord."
> Uncle John . . . greets each brother while Brother High beats his fists together and preaches the "word." Uncle John sits down on a split log, claps his big hairy hands and pats his brogan shoes on the puncheon floor and sanctions all Brother High says.

Women and men passed baskets of *good Baptist grub* among the people as they listened to the long sermons. Later the preachers ate at a special table set for them under the beech trees.

Uncle John, whose son had accused him of going to the *Association* mainly to show off his new teeth, found the *grub* and the new teeth the cause of considerable suffering: he choked on a bit of meat and could swallow nothing until the eleventh day when he coughed up the offending particle and proclaimed loudly that he had *whopped the Devil.* (His family had feared that they would have to take him home in a *wooden overcoat.*)

To a greater extent, perhaps, than any other religious gathering in the hills, the *Association* was a get-together where *saved* people *got happy* and *praised the Lord* long and loudly. It tended more to emphasize the pleasures of being Baptists than to stress the awful threat of hell-fire and damnation to sinners. The Baptist preachers tried to outdo one another in courtesies to their colleagues as well as in the length of their sermons. The women gave an all-out demonstration of their cooking and baking ability; and everyone fellowshiped in a spirit of the greatest generosity and mutual helpfulness.

A more frequent and popular church social was the *basket dinner,* or *dinner on the grounds.* When an all-day service made it practical, the women of the church prepared abundant food on Saturday for dinner on the church grounds preceding the evening preaching services. Like the *pie socials,* these were the scene of much laughing, talking, and courting among the young people—and, not infrequently, the scene of fights. The usual pattern when all ran smoothly was for the families to spread their picnic meal on the ground or for families to get together and share what their baskets contained, then for everyone to move about the churchyard and socialize, and finally go into the church house for the *meeting.*

Stuart has referred to *basket dinners* in several stories, but his only detailed account of one was much involved with a feud, and at least two families loaded their wounded into their wagons after bloody fighting and went home before the evening service. The story, nevertheless, illustrated the basic customs associated with the traditional hill *basket dinner.* Each family had brought abundant food, the best their larders afforded; each spread a tablecloth in the churchyard a slight distance from other families. The boys wearing their silk shirts and flashy ties hoped to *catch us some girls.* "Be a lot of good-lookin' girls there. Allus is at a basket dinner at the Gap Church."

The Dinguses feasted on

> . . . dumplings, pickles, cake, pie, ham, fried chicken, apple preserves, plum preserves, apricots, apples, corn-bread, biscuits, light-bread, jelly, Irish 'taters, sweet 'taters, squirrel, soup beans, green beans, leatherbritches beans, blackberry cobbler, raspberries, dewberries, strawberries, wild-plum jelly, wild-grape jelly. . . .

The older women usually exchanged news and gossip, and the men indulged in theological disputes as well as exchanging crop news. The women always hoped that no violence would take place, although it was not uncommon for members of certain families to attend the same small church for many years without speaking to one another, except in anger, as had the Dinguses and Bridgewaters of this story. Ma urged the Dinguses: ". . . Fill yourselves on good grub now and this evenin' we'll fill our hearts on the word of the Scriptures. Goin' to be some good preachin' in th' house this evenin'." A *basket dinner* was always a part of the Baptist Association, but other denominations also had basket dinners.

Equally exciting, but a more serious occasion, was the meeting in which a church member was threatened with excommunication, or in mountain speech *churched*. The exercising of strong disciplinary measures over the church members from seventeenth-century New England to modern times in certain churches has sometimes seemed harsh to those outside the church. By Stuart's time the regular monthly meeting of Baptists no longer took place (with all members present) to discipline those guilty of fighting, lying, and harmful gossip, stealing, adultery, horse racing, dishonest business dealings, and drunkenness; but in one or another of Stuart's stories every one of these sins has been dealt with. Frolicking and dancing, treating the church with contempt, and other ancient offenses have also received repeated mention in Stuart's writings. Not all offenses were serious enough to justify one's being *churched;* and, no matter how serious the offense, if the sinner repented with enough humility, the measure would serve as a purification rather than as a complete excommunication.

In Stuart's story "The Devil and Television" a man was *churched* for having a television set in his home. It might have occurred in this *Church of the Old-Fashioned Faith* for any of the other offenses mentioned in the following section of a sermon on "The Devil Has Many Faces":

> "The devil loves company and he is always with the crowd at these places of amusement. If he was there walking among these people they would run and scream. And God's Houses would be full and running over with people. But that's not the way the devil does things. He is a devil with many faces, visiting many places. And now the devil has the slickest way he has ever had of getting into the homes, homes of good people, religious people. He comes in this newfangled thing called television. I believe that's what it's called. I've never seen it. But these places of amusement, these singers and dancers and baseball players and wrestlers and women in shorts and low-necked dresses above the elbows are brought right inside the homes for the family to see. Brothers and Sisters, the devil has pulled a fast one."

Had Pa repented, as other backsliders had done, he would have fallen to his knees and prayed along with the Moderator and the congregation that his sins be forgiven, amid shouts of *Glory* and *Amen.* But Pa is a transitional figure and is not convinced of the sinfulness of his new diversion: " 'Come, let's go to your church for a change,' Pa said. 'I'm not movin' my television set out of our home. And I'm still goin' on to church.' " The usual procedure was to warn the offender in advance of the trial; preach a sermon against the specific sin of which the offender had been accused;

then call on the person to say "what he had to say for himself," giving him the opportunity to fall trembling to his knees; and finally to give the verdict, which in Pa's case would, of course, be excommunication. The story related that more than thirty of the sixty members of this group had been *churched,* but only Pa and one other had remained unrepentant. In "Weep No More, My Lady," Stuart attributed the practice of *churching* members for worldly pleasures (or the threat of doing so) to the Mountain Baptists, the purpose, of course, being to purify rather than to get rid of the member.

Whether a hill man had ever brought himself to the point of making a public confession of sin earlier in life and whether or not he had belonged to a religious body that practiced *churching* to keep its members on the straight-and-narrow path, he nearly always wanted to *cut the last rotten speck out of this good apple* when he felt the approach of death. The sins most often confessed on deathbeds were adultery, theft, and murder. Through dreams, the hearing of voices on the wind, or the visualizing of an embodiment of death, he seemed to know when the time had come for him to die. Only the rare exception was unconcerned in that extremity as to where he would spend eternity:

> Where will you spend eternity?
> The question comes to you and me!
> Tell me, what shall your answer be?
> Where will you spend eternity?
>
> Leaving the straight-and-narrow way,
> Going the downward road today,
> Sad will their final ending be,
> —Lost through a long eternity!
>
> Refrain
> ETERNITY! ETERNITY!

Lost through a long eternity!
Repent, believe this very hour,
Trust in the Saviour's grace and power,
Then will your joyous answer be
SAVED THROUGH A LONG ETERNITY!

Battle Keaton, for whom the song was sung, was counted *among the blest;* but not so fortunate, the hill people thought, were Annis Bealer and Old Harmon Manley who "died cussing the Lord." Old Man Slackburn, of course, was *saved,* for he "left the world a-clapping his hands and saying, 'Glory to God. They ain't no doubt now. I'm bound for the Promised Land. All you people meet me there.'"

Stuart's many stories and poems dealing with death and the folk beliefs and customs associated with it have reflected the hill man's continual awareness of its imminence and his acceptance of death with the same fatalism that he has accepted the hardships of life. Inseparable from folklore were the interpretations of birthmarks, *tokens,* heavenly visions, and the beliefs out of which the *settin'-up* and the *funeralizing* grew. The hill folk of the past would have associated all such matters with the *one true religion* of their *Old-Fashioned Faith.* Some of the customs relating to death and burial, like those in other phases of hill life, became dissociated from the beliefs out of which they developed and by Stuart's time were known simply as *the way of the hills.*

The behavior of family and neighbors at the time of a death in the Kentucky hills, as pictured in "Battle Keaton Dies," "300 Acres of Elbow Room," "Plowshare in Heaven," and "She Kept Her Distance," was typical of the culture. The death having been *norrated around,* neighbors came to wash, dress, and *lay out* the corpse (women if a woman had died, and men if the deceased were a man). Not often perhaps did these persons comment, as they did of old Battle

Keaton, that the water they had washed him in was "damn black" when they emptied the washtub over the bank from the back porch.

As mentioned earlier, every effort was made to comply with deathbed requests as to the details of the funeral and burial. In "She Kept Her Distance," Effie Pratt felt honored by the dying Lommie Wilburn's request that Effie prepare her for her casket: "I want you to wash me clean and put new clothes on me. . . . I don't want an undertaker to touch me." (An ironic detail suggesting, as Stuart often does, the transition at work in his region, was the fact that Lommie's son was an undertaker.) Battle Keaton's daughter, over the protest of some of her friends, honored old Battle's request that he be buried in his long underwear and a blue work shirt. Many agreed that she was doing the right thing, even though the coffin the five men down in the barn were making of wild-cherry and oak planks had to be worked over, so that only part of the lid could be opened and his long white drawers would not show.

The coffins were often shaped to fit the body: "It was shaped like a guitar-box," Billy Auxier said of his mother's homemade coffin. The coffin might be of cedar, poplar, or any other well-seasoned lumber that was available. As they did for the beautiful orphan girl Fern, the women lined the coffin when the men brought it to the house. "The girls went down in the hollow and gathered wreaths of the blue sandflower, goldenrod, and farewell-to-summer," and laid them around the room in which the person *laid a corpse*. A typical *settin'-up* appears in "She Kept Her Distance":

> People came by twos, tens, twenties. They came to sit up with the corpse. It was a custom here. They laughed and talked in the front room. They sang a hymn. They spoke of life. They spoke of crops to be planted. They did not talk about death. They kept the lamp burning low in the backroom with Lommie all night. . . .

In "Sittin' up with Grandma" and in "A Close Shave" the observance of this custom proved somewhat premature. Grandma *returned from the dead;* the man in "A Close Shave" who had been kicked by a mule could hear all that was said and see all that was done around him, but was unable to communicate the fact that he still lived until after he had been fully prepared for his coffin:

> Neighbors . . . telling her what a fine man and a good neighbor I'd been all my life. They told her that I was better off than their husbands who sat around the dining-room table looking at the white two-gallon jug with the long brown neck plugged with a corn-cob stopper.

The men talked of the dead before they began swigging from the jug. Meanwhile the young people played post office, and the sons and daughters quarreled over the division of their father's estate. During the midnight supper someone became aware of the *dead* man's movements. "Before sunrise," he said, "I had chopped up my coffin and made my will."

Some *settin'-ups* became rather disgraceful affairs, such as the one for Uncle Jeff, at which his drinking companions "tried to drown their cares and grief about Uncle Jeff's passing." Some were very quiet, like Phoeby's in "Plowshare in Heaven." Phoeby had a store-bought coffin with shiny handles. The house was filled with people, but they sat quietly around the big log fire, at times some of them breaking the silence or soft-spoken conversation to sing a favorite old hymn.

> There are two chairs in the back of the big front room. On these two chairs is the coffin. . . . It is a bluish-gray-colored coffin and it has a glass lid. . . . Phoeby is in the coffin. I know she is in the dress she told Mom about and she has the pennies that she covered with dark cloth over her eyes.

About four o'clock the people who had sat up during the night went home to do their morning chores, but others took their places. Many of the men did not go to the fields even in crop time or to their jobs on public works when a neighbor was *laying a corpse*.

The corpse was never left alone. It would have been difficult for an old-time hill man to express to an outsider exactly what he meant by *showing respect to the dead*, but Stuart has communicated the peculiar atmosphere of the *settin'-up* with its socializing in the foreground and always in the background a superstitious awe in the presence of a great mystery.

It is credible that someone of Stuart's acquaintance, like Flem in "Men of the Mountains," had stored several barrels of salt to preserve himself and his wife in their graves so that they would "keep like a jar of apples till the Judgment Day." But surely his tall-tale brand of humor prompted his account of six months of play parties at weekly *settin'-ups* for old Doug Grayhouse, salted down in the attic at age ninety-six, while relatives all over the country recovered from illnesses, bought new clothes, and otherwise made ready to attend the funeral on the money Grandpa had bequeathed to them for the purpose.

Waning of the prejudice against embalming and removing the corpse from the home before removal to the burial place has been reflected in the otherwise grotesque situation of competing undertakers rushing to the scene of a homicide in "Competition at Slush Creek." The old-fashioned *settin'-up*, or *wake*, with rare exceptions belongs to the past.

Another means of *showing respect for the dead* was the mountain funeral, such as Mrs. Auxier's: "Took three preachers four hours to preach Ma's funeral," said Billie. Equally long were the funeral sermons in "Fern," "Death and Decision," and *Taps for Private Tussie*. In the days before embalming, when deaths took place in remote sections of the hills, it was understandable that the *buryin'* took place with little ceremony, and the real memorial service was delayed until a minister could attend—or several ministers. In bad weather it was a considerable undertaking to get the body to the place of burial. In "I Remember Mollie" the husband sat on the coffin of his dead wife to keep it from bouncing off the wagon, and the people following in the funeral procession were splashed with mud from the chugholes in the rough country road. In "Death and Decision" the male descendants carried Old Dad to the *newfangled deadwagon,* the ambulance that waited at the main road. In *Taps* six stout Tussie men carried the coffin all the way up the steep mountainside in the heat of summer.

A more unusual custom in the northeastern Kentucky hills has been the *funeralizing* that memorialized a person long dead or paid respect to the same person repeatedly, as in Stuart's story "Weep No More, My Lady." In this story a man who had been funeralized each year on the anniversary of his first funeral was being honored for the seventh time by his Mountain Baptist wife. Her second husband, at first acting *like a sheep that had got into the wrong pasture,* mellowed under the influence of the mountain whisky that circulated freely during the service, and by the end of it, was mourning along with his wife for his predecessor.

The *funeralizing* began at the house with a period of *fellowshiping*, singing, and taking inventory of past conduct under the threat of being *churched*. When no one confessed to making love to another man's wife, gambling, or attending street fairs, circuses, or picture shows, the first part of the service ended with everyone's singing "Leaning on the Everlasting Arms." Then all ate a hearty dinner before climbing up the steep mountain to the graveside.

When everyone reached the burial spot, Sister Ebbie lined out the hymn "From Greenland's Icy Mountains" to the accompaniment of Brother Amos' wailing guitar. The preacher,

The gathering broke up amid much "handshaking and slapping each other on the back," while everybody tried to talk at the same time and "everybody was happy in fellowship and love." The suggestion of transition was expressed by Pa's children at the beginning of the story: ". . . I don't see any use having his funeral preached every year. It brings back old memories. And it brings back old griefs." Pa had been a *strong* Mountain Baptist who *got a token* of his approaching death, went to the barn, and made his coffin of seasoned boards he had kept there in case of a death in the family, and cleared the place in the thicket where he wanted to be buried. Ma insisted on having the *funeralizing:* ". . . if we didn't have the funeral preached every year, he'd turn over in his grave."

Stuart has given only brief attention to the old custom of *cleaning up the burial grounds.* Subrinea Tussie and Tarvin Bushman set aside a day to clean away the weeds from the final resting place of her people under the trees of heaven in the squatters' graveyard:

> Tarvin cuts the briars with his hoe. He whacks them down. He rakes them from the graves with his hoe. He picks up armloads of briars and carries them from this ancient graveyard. . . . Subrinea gets down on her knees and places bits of torn sod back in place. She pulls weeds from the graves. She lays bunches of wild roses, dusty miller, wild trillium, blue ageratum, bloodroot, and eggplant on the graves. She pushed the dead leaves away from the head stones.

Subrinea's feeling "like I just haf to decorate my people's graves" is typical among the hill people. In most families or communities it would have been an all-day social occasion with many helping and perhaps with dinner on the grounds.

The importance of looking after the dead was vivid in

Stuart's memories of his own family: of his small brothers being hauled in bad weather the long country miles to be buried on land owned by his grandfather; later, of his father's having them moved to the Plum Grove Churchyard so that the whole family could *sleep* there together (less than a year later his father was buried there beside them).

Throughout the mountains it has been a matter of the utmost concern to a family for their dead to receive *decent burial.* Whatever confusion of flesh and spirit, whatever of superstition and sentimentality may have influenced these customs, Stuart has pictured their integral place in the culture of northeastern Kentucky.

Stuart has clearly demonstrated his awareness of the bad effects of bigotry and superstition in hill religion; but humor has everywhere dominated protest. He has mentioned the midweek prayer service and Sunday services not interrupted by the excitement of a practical joker impersonating God or free-for-all fighting in the churchyard; but the extreme incidents, in his opinion, make better *yarns.* He has sometimes, but not always, rationalized the hill man's views. He has understood the need of his people for the emotional outlet of the hill revival, but he fully recognizes the suggestibility of the fiery sermons that can mislead as often as lead. His own family respected the deathbed requests that his father made in 1954, but they were reasonable. At times he has seemed regretful at the passing of old neighborly customs, as the hill people have toned down their church activities and accepted the services of professional morticians. The over-all impression, however, has been good-humored tolerance of both old and new.

CHAPTER THREE

The Hill Man's Pleasures and the Code of the Hills

. . . we who have loved life, fought, kissed,
played, worked, loved and hated. . . .

MEN OF THE MOUNTAINS

The figures of earth who people Stuart's poems and stories
have little acquaintance with Lum Dryasdust. Their pleasures were diversified and overlapped with almost every
other phase of their living. If these pleasures sometimes
offended the lowland sense of morality and propriety, they
seldom violated the code of the hills. At elections, court ses-
sions, the jockey grounds, workings, and church socials, in
contests of poker-faced shrewdness and in tests of physical
strength, the hill men looked on with cool mountain eyes,
spoke with dry mountain humor, were *dangerous as a
cocked gun* when angered, and played always to win. In the
heyday of the folk community the people made their own
recreation with the same self-sufficiency as they raised their
bread. What Stuart has said of their economic standard was
equally true of their leisure-time activities—if they were
poor, they did not know it. Hill parties, hunting and fishing,
singing and tale telling, eating, drinking, fighting, and love-
making varied the routine of work.

91

Workin's, which had been of vital importance in the truly pioneer period, were largely social affairs by Stuart's lifetime. The events were *norrated* by the *grapevine telephone;* and people of all ages walked, rode mules, went in jolt wagons to *molasses-makings, corn-shuckings, apple-peelings, bean-stringings,* and other such *gatherin's.* Usually these workings ended in play-party games such as *Skip to My Lou,* in party games such as *Button, Button, Who's Got the Button;* and *Post Office* for the younger people, or in square dancing to fiddle, banjo, and guitar music. Stuart attended such parties with his students during his first year as a high-school teacher.

In many ways the sorghum molasses-making in *Trees of Heaven* was typical of these hill *frolics.* Most of the work had been done in advance, leaving only the final barrel of sorghum for the *stir-off,* enough to give the *champean lassie-maker* an opportunity to demonstrate his skill and the young people a chance to gather around the pan of boiling cane juice and feed one another the sweet white foam on paddles whittled from willow wood—and a chance to push the obstreperous ones into the sticky, sour-smelling, waist-deep *skimmin' hole,* with no regard for his blue serge pants, white shirt, and low-cut slippers. It gave the old people a break in the routine of work and an opportunity to exchange news and gossip of the countryside.

A few steps from the cane mill, beside the pile of cane stalks, was a platform of oak planks resting on heavy oak sleepers. Lanterns at each of the four corners provided light for dancing. Tarvin was carrying the last of the cane stalks to the mill, his mother Fronnie was feeding them into the burrs, and his father Anse was stirring the molasses in the sorghum pan when the approaching sound of "Down in the Valley" and the notes of fiddles, guitars, and banjos heralded the coming of their neighbors and friends.

"The way they sing it seems like there must be a whole army of singin', dancin', and fun-lovin' people," Anse Bushman remarked.

> The old mix and mingle. They talk about crops, chickens, cattle, hogs, and next year's crops. The young mix and mingle and talk about love, and they don't talk about anything much. They feed each other foam and laugh. They slap each other on the back and laugh, and the boys slap the girls little light love licks, and take them by the arms and fondle them lightly.

Boliver Tussie stirred off the last pan of molasses with expert skill, dipping the green scum from the pan with a dipper in one hand while he pushed the amber currents through the divisions of the pan with a stir in the other hand, keeping the juice moving and not letting it stay too long in any one division of the pan. Anse meanwhile placed the last barrel under the plug, lifted the plug, and let the golden current drain. Immediately after the pan was emptied, washtubs of cold water were poured into the pan to keep the furnace fire beneath it from scorching the pan bottom.

While the musicians played *Birdie* from their split-log bandstand, couples of all ages formed eight sets of four couples each, and the *caller* began the figures for *Cage the Bird.*

> . . . The sweat pours from the young couples' brown faces and it runs and drips from the old men's beards. The music is lively and there are laughter, talking, and squeals from the dancing couples as the music goes fast and furious. Anse steps lively in his big brogan shoes; sparks fly from the hobnails on his shoe soles when he leaps in the air and comes down on the hard planks . . . . He lets out a big "Whoopee."

When pretty Subrinea Tussie's squatter-timber-cutter cousin tried to take her away from Tarvin, Bollie landed in the skimming hole, for Tarvin hit him a *deadner*. As soon as Bollie was able, he staggered homeward with the thick green cane juice dripping from his best clothes, looking *as if the frogs had been roostin' on him*. The men *hiked*, spit, and drank from the jugs of moonshine their host had provided, the kind that would *make you love your neighbor as you love yourself*. They left the jugs on the cane pile while they danced. The young people hugged and kissed on the dance floor. The sleepy younger children rested on the cane pile.

When the stars began to fade into the morning sky, the children were awakened, and the crowd—still singing, laughing, swearing, hollering, went home to begin another day of hard work.

The *corn-shucking* described in *Hie to the Hunters*, although its involvement with Mr. Hargis' attempt to take his runaway boy home from the hills kept it from being typical, showed several traditional aspects of this *working*. A fifteen-acre field of corn on Buzzard Roost had a permanent dance floor built on a level spot down in the ravine, since the family made a corn-shucking "the big social event of the year in the Plum Grove hills." The couples walked and rode into the hollow, the single girls riding in the saddle and the boys with their arms around the girls guiding the mules and horses; the married women clinging on behind their husbands who rode in the saddle (possibly expressing truth as well as wry humor).

In the cornfield each couple had about four shocks to shuck with the homemade shucking pegs the men had whittled from seasoned hickory. These pegs had straps of leather or groundhog skin that fitted neatly over the back of the hand. When a boy found a red ear of corn, he kissed his girl, following old tradition. The girls' bright cotton dresses and the boys' brightly striped and checked shirts and red bandannas made the cornfield a colorful scene under the big *wagon-wheel moon.* The glint of pistols sticking from their holsters, Sparkie attributed to the hill boy's taste in decoration; but they were also reminders of never-absent danger from wild animals and human enemies.

As previously mentioned, fights were the rule rather than the exception at hill gatherings; but an all-out battle with corn stubble and pumpkins, such as crowded out the traditional dance at the Sparks' corn-shucking, is hyperbole—the more effective because it dramatizes the barrier between the hill people and intruders from the outside.

Each *working* had its unique characteristics, but all had in common the gay socializing of old and young in play-work. Certain families did not attend these *wild frolickings* because they thought the drinking, fighting, and general boisterousness were *trashy,* but these *stuck-up things* bothered the merrymakers not at all!

Stuart's accounts of the *bellin' o' the bride* tuned in on one of the gayest and noisiest of hill frolics. His young people mingled their voices with the jingling of cowbells as they huddled happily in blankets on a *doodle* of hay in a mule-drawn sleigh. As they scrambled about the premises of the bride's home, the boys threatened loudly to ride the groom on a rail. The newlyweds hid comfortably within earshot of their serenaders, who made the winter night echo with young voices, fox horns, bells, clanking plow points, rattling pans, tubs, and buckets. At intervals pistols and shotguns barked harmlessly at the moon. Then it was time to take the party inside where the warmth of mountain hospitality made up for any lack of comfort or convenience. The merrymakers had access to a sixty-gallon keg of hard cider, sixteen-gallon kegs of moonshine, cherry wine, strawberry wine, and blackberry wine. The taste-bud tobacco for chewing, twists of home-grown burley for smoking, and cigars were passed in a washtub and a split-bottom feed

basket; the candy, *popcorn and 'lassie balls* in a dishpan.
The men carried the furniture from the front room to clear
it for dancing, and the merrymaking continued until dawn.

The old people talked of their own bellings, sometimes
participated in the dancing, sometimes sat back, patted
their feet, and clapped their hands in time to the music.
Uncle Bill-Ike compares nostalgically the *bellin's* and
dances of his youth with those of the time of the newlyweds
of the story, but probably parties of both generations sometimes got out of hand:

> "When I was a boy . . . people enjoyed themselves
> more than they do today. W'y you can't have a dance
> here but what somethin' happens. Lights shot out. Some-
> body gets plugged before daylight. Somebody gets knifed.
> Something happens every time we have a dance."

In "Kentucky Hill Dance" and in *Hie to the Hunters* Stuart has described square dances held for their own sake,
parties which he has pictured as scenes of noisy fun never
free from the danger of fighting, in itself one of the hill
man's pleasures.

One Stuart character said with characteristic hill droll-
ery, *hit some people with a sour apple and they get drunk,*
but more than a sour apple was provided at most hill gatherings. It was not without reason that a hill woman sometimes looked at her man and said, *the Devil is in his broth
a-brewin'. Rotten stuff mixed with carbide and coppers* or
even the *pure corn licker* with its crystal bead could make a
man *douncy,* and in sufficient quantities make him *drunk as
a biled owl,* or even give him the *blind billiards.* Wherever
hill men gathered, drinking and fighting were almost sure to
take place, even at the religious gatherings. Stuart has many
times pictured this darker side of hill pleasures, as in the
following poem:

Who would believe that Shooting Charlie Paul
Was hauled out on this hill after a brawl?
Am Sickler shot him at the Hood-Run dance.
Am knew better than to take a chance.
He was hemmed in—victim of circumstance.
He was stabbed twice with Charlie Paul's dull knife;
But he tore loose and at a frightful chance
He drove a bullet through Charlie Paul's lung.
Charlie Paul fell to death at twenty-one.
Charlie Paul had two notches on his gun.
Am Sickler went and served his year in the pen
And Charlie Paul is sleeping under clay.

They'll fight at the drop of a hat, and they'll drop it themselves. As Uncle Uglybird Skinner and Pa reminisced of their own youth, the former recalled losing his sweetheart because of his *drinkin' and carvartin' and carryin' on with the boys,* who *toted* pistols and entertained themselves on a Sunday afternoon by shooting all over the countryside at snakes, lizards, or nothing. "Every young buck wanted the fastest hoss, the best pistil, and the purtiest gal!" Pa recalled.

The fighting methods and tactics varied. Some *cut drive* with their fists and landed a haymaker that was almost enough to *salivate* the victim, as Tarvin Bushman struck Bollie Beaver. Some were content to smear a rival in his best clothes by hitting him *casouse* with tomatoes, peaches, and the like, as in "Vacation in Heaven," when a young man had the misfortune to wear a white suit to call on a hill girl in strange territory (the white suit was a *flowerpot* for their pistols). Some who *carried the difference* or the *balance of power* in the form of a gun were quick on the trigger, sometimes shooting from the hip, and the victim fell *relaxed like a squirmin' black snake with its head cut off.* Some were *bad'ns to knife:* ". . . Brother Tim and Candy got in that cuttin' scrape with the Tinsleys. Tim got his right eye cut out, and Candy got his juggle vein nicked a little and a couple of cuts to the holler. But he lived." If no better weapon offered—or if guns and knives had been ruled out in certain fights—it was possible to *brain* a foe with a *sled standard,* as the Bridgewaters did when they killed Pa Dingus in "The Basket Dinner."

Many of the fights began over girls, often not the kind who were *women for a livin',* the kind hill men needed for wives. References to courtship and love-making in Stuart's writing range from idealistic and poetic self-expression to crass sensualism, trickery, and vulgarity.

Hill romances often began when a boy walked a girl home from church or a church social, enjoying the miles and the pauses at the *drawbars* up into some lonely hollow. Others began at parties, and some at hangings or even at funerals. Bashful at first in conversation, the hill girls were usually quick to lose their reserve when alone with a boy and were seldom unreceptive to his kisses and embraces (a jealous snooper called their love-making *gum-sucking* in one story). In spite of the opinion of some of the older women that a girl who would kiss a boy in the presence of others was *a little loose with herself,* young couples were likely to be *all loved up* on an excursion train returning from a hanging, in a sled returning from a belling, or beside the well gum in the girl's front yard where they said good night. The mountain girls did not consider sixteen at all young for marriage, and some married even younger. Once a girl had accepted a boy's attentions, it was almost sure to cause a fight if she permitted attentions from another. *A man that won't fight fer his woman ain't got the right color of blood in his veins* was a firm tenet in the hill code. Yet, it was the girl who was *ruint* if she were left to bear a *woods colt* while the father of her child lost himself *somewhere in the West.* No particular stigma seemed to be attached to premarital pregnancy if the couple married afterward.

Sometimes a girl scorned a would-be suitor with the disparaging folk expression, *I wouldn't have him if his head was strung with gold.* The folk metaphor is often barnyard associated. A person who had made a bad marriage was said to have *driv (druv) her ducks (his goose) to a bad market,* and the usual attitude was that if a person had *burned a blister he had to sit on it.* When marriages seemed likely to end in separations, the old people said, *looks like the quill is a-goin' to split.* If a widow renewed her interest in men, *her comb was a-gettin' red.* Always, in and out of marriage, *when you dance you've got to pay the fiddler.* Sensible girls, of course, knew when they had found *a nice man to tie to,* and were not slow to *jump the broomstick.*

In *Trees of Heaven* Stuart's poetic naturalness in presenting the scene between Tarvin Bushman and Subrinea Tussie after they had worked together all night with the *lambing* is untouched by ugliness. Tarvin, who told the girl that he had never *known any gal* except her, considered himself married to her; and through her "learned to laugh, to work and play . . . volcanic outburst of Nature that she is." Not all such affairs led to marriage: in "A Bad Disease" the beautiful squatter girl ran away with a cross-eyed undertaker and stayed long enough to contract a venereal disease, which she brought back to her mountain lover; Old Alec's daughter Sue, who left home during World War II to work in the city, returned with an illegitimate child, and he received her as if she had been a war casualty. Few hill parents in Stuart's fiction or in real life refused to take a jilted girl back into the home.

Many poems and stories have dealt with adultery, and several with homicide resulting from guilty passion, notably in "I Remember Mollie" and "A Land Beyond the River." In the former a man poisoned his wife so that he could be free to take another man's wife; but he went to the penitentiary instead. In the latter, the husband who murdered his rival went free and took to another community his beautiful lonely wife whom he still loved. In a lighter vein, "A Yard of String" described a brawl that began as a birthday surprise party and moved through the stages of dancing, drinking, and playing kissing games until jealous husbands and wives became enraged. *Fine and Superfine,* a game in which pawns were redeemed by *making a telephone, measuring three yards of ribbon, chewing a yard of string,* and other kissing forfeits, drove the men to throwing whisky bottles and in general to tearing up the party, and led the wives to maneuver their husbands out into the fresh air and on the way home. In most stories and some poems dealing with adultery and illicit love Stuart has achieved a grim or grotesque humor; yet some characters, such as Vittie Tussie in *Taps* and Subrinea in *Trees,* are involved with social criticism and tragic pathos.

Most mountain men wanted *a decent wife* when they decided to marry. In the hills, as elsewhere in American society, chastity was more often lauded in women than in men; but with surprising frequency both the unfaithful wives and husbands were forgiven in Stuart's stories.

In his fiction Stuart has often worked into the dialogue little intolerances and frustrating differences that alienate husband and wife or that corrode and kill love. Wives have irritated and embarrassed their *weaked* stubborn husbands by praying in public for them to *get saved,* nagging them to stop drinking *rotgut moonshine* before they *get snakes in their boots,* or henpecking them in innumerable small ways to vent their own vague discontent. Men who spent long hours at the plow or in the timber too seldom sensed their lonely women's need for poetry in their lives.

Stuart's focus is sharp and sudden, picturing the moment of truth that sets a tone of incessant friction or, more happily, of forgiving affection for two lives together. His is not the subtle probing into complexities and ambiguities so dear to writers such as Edith Wharton and Henry James. His vein is rich in another way. He has spotlighted in hundreds of vividly realized episodes the hill way with love triangles, domestic conflicts, and reconciliations. Some, like "Whip-poor-Willie," "Woman in the House," and "Hair" are keyed to low comedy. "I Remember Mollie," "Land Beyond the River," and "Toes" for all their humor have tragic pathos. "Henpecked," "Rain on Tanyard Hollow," and "The Storm" are comfortably resolved.

The love story takes the melody line in a hill symphony of changing seasons in *Trees of Heaven,* a novel pulsing with mountain life and work. The later *Daughter of the Legend* tells a more idyllic love story in a less exuberant novel.

Stuart's poetry has often captured the wonder and the beauty of young love—and the pain, too. His John and Kathaleen sequence in *Album of Destiny* and his personal poems in *Hold April!* are proof enough that he can treat love themes seriously and delicately.

Whether he deals with the ludicrous antics of adolescent courtship, the grotesque comedy of freakishly mismatched couples, the stoic acceptance of relationships that cannot be changed, the springtime sweetness of young love, or the autumn warmth of comfortable marriage, Jesse Stuart's writings reflect fully the virtues and vices of man-woman relationships that have made literature in all times and places.

The hill man's taste for fighting and his jealousy in love were facets of a keenly competitive nature. His fights were by no means limited to those growing out of love affairs, and his love for competition was by no means limited to fighting. He enjoyed contests between man and man, between man and animal, and between animal and animal. The short story "The Champion" is based on the pride certain hill men took in their capacity for food. Sam Whiteapple's *nail keg* of a stomach did not protest when he *winned the eatin' championship* on Raccoon Creek by eating a hog's head or when he *et* five stewed hens on Uling Branch; but when he put whole grains of corn down his *gullet* in competition with a rooster, he not only lost the contest but had to live for a time on corn flakes!

In the category of events that happened at least once and probably *only* once were certain offbeat contests, in some of which Stuart seemed to be symbolizing traits and conditions of his people or of universal human nature. In "Nest Egg" a scrub rooster that was not wanted or expected was driven from the barn lot by the other roosters and had to scratch in the hills for his living; nevertheless he grew into a champion fighter. Then at the peak of his fame he was ingloriously killed by a little screech owl that caught him off guard on his roost in the barn one night. A hill dog put an end to an illegal gambling enterprise and made a small fortune for his owner by killing a wildcat in "Fight Number Twenty-five." The underdog won by the clever trick of dodging the cat's lunge at him and then springing onto the wildcat's back and cracking his thin skull.

Uncle Op Akers' yarns, with their usual tall-tale flavor, used names of people who were well known in the community and definite settings as to time and place. Such a story was the basis for Stuart's "Goin' to th' Buttin'." In the days when Teddy Roosevelt was President, according to Op, a crowd of people gathered on Laurel Ridge to watch Minton Artner butt against a ram. Minton, a short bullish man with *shoulders as broad as a corncrib door,* a small head, and a short, thick neck, had injured many people by butting them. Minton outwitted the ram by jumping behind a tree and letting the ram break his neck by butting against the tree, and some of the people objected that Minton had not *butted fair.*

In "No Hero," a story having its background in the depression 1930s, Stuart used a favorite theme of having the underdog win fairly but cleverly. The *tall as a bean pole* Hester King won five dollars per minute by gentling a bear instead of wrestling with him, using knowledge he had acquired as a cordwood cutter in the upper peninsula of Michigan: he knew that a bear liked to be rubbed between the ears and on the stomach, but only a man too skinny for the bear to embrace could have escaped injury long enough to apply that knowledge.

In "One of the Lost Tribe" a boy closely resembling Jesse Stuart at that age killed a snake with his bare hands, choked a groundhog that *come nigh as a pea tearing his guts out,* and killed a bull that had attacked school children—killed it with a hickory club after he had got it under control by grabbing the horns and putting his toes in the bull's nostrils. He could *put the cat on* boys bigger than himself who called him a *stinkin' Republican,* and earned himself the admiring hill exclamation: "Lord, but that's a game boy." This story illustrates the hill man's unshakable loyalty to his political party, evident even in the boy far too young to vote, the *fightinest* boy in the country.

The love of contests made the Fourth-of-July and Labor-Day celebrations in Greenup popular with the Red Necks from the surrounding countryside. Stuart's description of a Labor-Day celebration in the 1930s was probably typical. The streets were roped off for dancing and the contests. The latter included climbing a greased pole with the two-dollar-bill prize pinned to the top, catching the greased pig, sack races, wheelbarrow races, foot races, nail-driving, hog-calling (*Pig—ee—Pig-o-eee!*), cow-calling (*Swouke cow— Swoukee!*), and dancing contests. Prizes were also given to the prettiest girl, the man with the most children by one mother, the most loving couple, and the man with the biggest foot. Throughout the day dancing, music, shouting, laughing, and drinking *Kentucky mountain dew* continued. A moonshiner was arrested, his load of eighty-six gallons of *good stuff that won't burn a man's guts* poured down over the riverbank; he feared that he could no longer avoid federal imprisonment at Atlanta, Georgia. A few were put in jail for disorderly conduct, but most of the celebrants went happily homeward at the end of the day eagerly anticipating the next occasion. The Greenup people looked upon the celebration as belonging to a "crude world of pistol-toting, moonshine-drinking, and fist-fighting mountaineers."

Stuart's description of a *frog-trouncin' contest* seems to have recorded a narrowly local custom that now belongs to the past. Possibly Stuart elaborated upon one of the Labor-Day festival contests to honor it as *Frog-Trouncin' Day*. The related but rather different sport of *frog-sticking* may have inspired the trouncing, but gave the frogs a better chance of survival. More probable is the persistence in the back country of a game Elizabethans called "filliping the toad." Thiselton-Dyer, in *Folklore in Shakespeare* (1883), describes the game in recognizable detail. Stuart country frog trouncers did it this way:

> The frog trouncer was a heavy plank balanced on a wooden horse like a teeter-totter. On one end the toad frog was placed and was tied there . . . with a white thread. The man trouncin' the frog hit the other end of the trouncer with his mallet and it sent the frog toward the sky and when the frog fell to the ground it was dead as four o'clock. One had to hit the trouncer exactly right to send the frog straight into the air; if he didn't hit it right, the frog would go sidewise.

Young Jake Hornbuckle, who won the contest in the story, had an especially heavy mallet whittled from a tough-butted white oak, filled with buckshot (in an inch auger hole stopped with an oak glut), and with a *yaller locust* handle. His frog went over the treetops completely out of sight; and he won the prize of a yearling bull.

The courthouse square in the county seat was a busy spot at which the country people gathered on Saturday afternoons, Sales Days (the first Monday in each month), and Court Days as well as on holidays. The old men sat trying to *whittle the longest shaving* and spun their *big windy tales* (the shaving was most acceptable when whittled from elm wood). Uncle Sweeter Dabney, broken-down blueblood though he was, brought his fiddle to the square and played for the Red Necks to dance in the street. Blind Frailey and his wife sang the old-time ballads to fiddle accompaniment. Sister Spence preached in the square urging sinners to repent and be saved.

Not far away from the square—or from any other hill gathering of importance any day—was the *jockey ground* where the horse traders matched their wits, and took keen pride without a qualm of conscience in *uptripping* another sharp trader. Happy was the man who got rid of a *heavie horse* or one with the *thumps* or a *hot-collared* or *cold-collared mule*. In "Rich Men" and "Horse-Trading Trembles" Stuart's accounts of trickery in hill trading reached tall-tale proportions: in the former, a trader disguised himself as a ragged beggar and then tore the money from a patch on his pants when the trade was definite; in the latter, a boy dyed a horse's mane, brushed his teeth, and used sponges to conceal the fact that the horse had the *heaves*— told the truth on the grounds, and no one believed him until after the trade. The hill code approved of this kind of shrewd business acumen and made no association of sharp trading with dishonesty.

The code of the hill man, as previously noted, developed during the era of his isolation, and retained into the twentieth century certain tenets that had largely disappeared elsewhere with the vanishing frontier. When that code deviated from lowland custom and the law, the deviations nearly always had their inception in fierce clan pride or the struggle for survival: for example, the lawsuits, the election procedures, the feuds, and the moonshining. Much of what may have appeared to the outlander as picturesque—if at times deplorable—custom the hill man looked upon as necessity.

On Court Days the most common cases involved broken *ar-tickles* between landlords and tenants, trouble over land titles, moonshining, carrying firearms, and the misdemeanors and felonies growing out of these and other things. Tense though the atmosphere sometimes got in the courtroom, and foul with tobacco smoke, whisky breaths, and the gamy smell of dirty clothes and unwashed bodies, the country people attended when they possibly could. It was a big social occasion for them. Women sat on the long benches, many of them with nursing babies. Men on the outside cursed the lawyers. "People love to hear a trial. Lovers meet each other here. Men come to talk about their crops. They come to swap horses. They come to trade and drink together. They come to have a good time." As Stuart has described the procedure, the judge took matters quite casually, almost everyone in the courtroom took sides, profanity and incriminations became vitriolic, and clan loyalty and influence overrode other considerations. Stuart's personal involvement in court procedures during his term as county superintendent (thirty-two lawsuits during a single year) gave him ample background for courtroom scenes in fiction. After Stuart had been struck with a blackjack, the man who assaulted him was brought before the Grand Jury. Armed men, *beardy-faced* and grim, were present to see that Stuart received no further injury—his own people from the hills and their friends. Although it was reasonably well established that the man had struck with intent to kill, he was fined only $200 and given no jail sentence.

A stubborn unreasoning strain in hill character enabled the hill people to rationalize lying under oath and evasion of man-made laws. Likewise, the hill people justified their political code. They could rationalize empty campaign promises, falsification of records, lying, and downright treachery if it helped their side to win. Kentuckians enjoy a colorful election, win or lose.

In "Thirty-Two Votes before Breakfast" Al Caney cast thirty-two votes in thirty-two precincts under thirty-two different names before he was apprehended. In "The People Choose" young Dusty Boone pretended to have received scars in feud battles, lied to both sides, and justified his deceit by ending a long-standing feud. In "Governor Warburton's Right-Hand Man" matters took an unexpected turn when the neutral narrator of the story received the political plum that both sides had expected. Political corruption emerged frequently and comically in *Taps for Private Tussie*. In "A Member of the Lost Tribe," "Uncle Casper," and "Road Number One" (among others) politics played a prominent part. A good deal of *rippin' and stavin'* went on at elections, and moonshine flowed freely. Few Kentuckians, hill or otherwise, have ever *tried to carry water on both shoulders*. Each has considered himself a strong Republican or Democrat (*so strong he stunk*), a member of the *Right Party* who voted *on the Lord's Side*.

The same code that held a man to his political party through thick and thin demanded fierce loyalty to his clan and stern justice by his own hand if the law was not on his side. Stuart has expressed this rigid code in the poem entitled "Boliver Cremeans Speaks of Justice," the justice being revenge upon the man who had stabbed his young brother to death and served only five years in prison for it:

> Since Chad must serve forever and a day
> Bruce Skeens will not return to visit kin,
> Scene of his crime and grave of one's slain;
> Both night and day one has been hidden in
> Rockcliffs and sprouts, waiting for him in vain.

> Since he won't come to us, we'll go to him
> With mountain justice from our stubborn clan;
> His knifing blood from us is woe for him . . .
> We take *an eye for eye, a man for man.* . . .

Stuart's peacemaking inclinations have been implicit in his handling of feuding themes. Yet he has ever been quick to retaliate when attacked by an enemy, and he has paid rich tribute in both prose and poetry to his hard-fighting ancestors. Although he could see the deplorable aspects of the mountain feud, he could also understand the unbending pride and the inflexible clan loyalty which were its seed ground. He has probably been an *oddling* in preferring poetry to blows, but his peace like that of his forbears always has had to be a peace with honor. In at least two of his stories, "The People Choose" and "Hell's Acre," he has made such a feud ending seem possible.

In "The People Choose" Subrinea Boone and Roosevelt Reffitt of feuding families fell in love at sight when they met at a *pie supper,* but Subrinea felt that nothing must happen to break the truce the two families had achieved by an even number of killings on each side: "It would take thirty years to try all the trials betwixt our families . . . it would take all of Kentucky's National Guards stationed at the courthouse the thirty years it took to try these cases." Dusty Boone settled this feud by scheming to get the support of both clans to elect him prosecuting attorney, by dismissing all indictments, persuading the two clan leaders to help him carry out a wager to roll the losing candidate down the hill in a barrel, and giving his blessing to the young lovers whose marriage would unite the two families.

In "Hell's Acre" the feud over a line fence began in 1918 and had cost the Hillmans $1,500 by 1928 when Pa decided that powder and lead were cheaper than lawyers' fees and court costs. The surviving members of both families had lost limbs and had *white swellin'* in their legs or nicked bones and internal injuries. In 1929 Adger Hillman announced to his beloved Effie Sturgin of the enemy family: "Look how our neighbors air gettin' ahead of us over behind the ridges. They air raisin' terbacker and corn while we are raisin' hell. When we marry, Effie, it will be ended. We'll all be kinfolks then." After they had *run like two turkeys* up the road out of sight and walked five miles to get their marriage license, then six miles to Brother Tobbie Bostick's and *jumped the broom,* Adger's prophecy came true, for neither family would fight their *kinfolks.* The worthless acre was divided between the two families.

The implication of both stories was the willingness of all concerned to stop fighting if they could do so without losing face.

In "Bury Your Dead" the marriage between members of the feuding families did not have such a happy outcome. Ceif Wampler, who never had been good to work, married Portia Pratt, whose father worked every man on his place to his utmost capacity. After fathering several children, Ceif died, and a grim farce ensued. His corpse was shuttled back and forth between the two families, neither of whom claimed him. The burial—but not the feud—was settled by having each family dig half of the grave, and Ceif was buried on the line between the two farms, half on the Pratt side and half on the Wampler side. This tale is typical of Stuart's indirect social protest of these darker aspects of hill life.

"The Basket Dinner" also ended with a temporary cessation of fighting because of injuries on both sides, but the feud went on. In this a third family became involved when Big William Hawthorne went to the *basket dinner* with Rilda Dingus, and won the day against great odds by *bushwacking* in a new way: he pinched the back of the neck of each Bridgewater who pursued him into the sprout thicket, offsetting the Bridgewaters' gains achieved by throwing *sled standards*. This tale of romance and fighting communicated the local color of a *basket dinner on the church grounds,* which usually ended with going inside the *church house* to hear a sermon. Each family spread a cloth and put on it bountiful amounts of fried chicken, cake, pie, and other picnic foods; after eating, the families usually mingled and socialized. Here, as in so many instances, Stuart has selected for a story the atypical instance of a traditional hill social custom.

"Death Has Two Good Eyes" and "Land of our Enemies" seem to be variants on the same basic situation: a clan leader in the Big Sandy community late in life married a woman of the opposing side and had by her a second large family. In the former he died in the *privy* of his home with the second wife, and his sons by his first wife waged bloody battle with rocks, clubs, and fists (guns and knives were tabu since their feuding half-brothers were *kinfolks*) in order to take his body home to their mother's house. In the second, he was clubbed to death by the enemy clan after a separation from his second wife, and had to be buried at night to avoid an all-out clan war at the funeral. No preacher or songs marked his burial, just a farewell volley of rifle shots fired over the grave by soldier comrades: "He has fit through a long war in the land of his enemies and he has fit well."

The story of Grandfather Mitch Stuart related in *Beyond Dark Hills* almost surely was the basis for the two stories just mentioned. Having *got saved* in a hill Methodist church he stayed in the church one week. Then he said: "I can't stand this sort of a life. I've got to live. I've got to have my licker and my terbacker. And I can't be a brother to a Houndshell." He remarried after his first wife died, and almost froze to death one winter night while he stayed in a log house near the road holding a double-barreled shotgun pointed through a crack waiting for a man that he suspected of coming to see his wife.

> And Grandpa did die on Big Sandy. We don't know how he died. We didn't know that he was dead until he was dead and buried. We heard that he was beaten to death . . . and the suspect sleeps under the Big Sandy clay not far away from Grandpa.

Stuart ends his "Elegy to Mitch Stuart":

> Old Mitch's a-fightin' still,
> He's got 'em on the run . . .
> One hand is on his bottle,
> The other on his gun.

The poet felt that if his lusty old grandfather, who was never free from clan wars, could have spoken his own epitaph he would have said: "I have no regrets, for I lived my life. I loved it. . . . I lived by the sword and by gad I can die by it."

When Stuart wrote of feuds, as when he wrote of other dark happenings in the hills, he thought of the transience of man-made troubles and of the renewing power of the earth that outlasts them. He ended a poem that told of twelve men's deaths in a single encounter at a hill dance with this contrast of transience and endurance:

> Flow gently, Sandy, with tears, blood, and sorrow,
> It is not long that mountain widows wait;
> Bull-tongues will snap the newground roots tomorrow
> While time plods on through centuries of hate.

As Stuart recalls his heritage of drink and gun, he considers it ultimately "an evil chance," for "to kill a man there is no victory won."

Stuart's depiction of moonshiners has shown the same ambivalence that has emerged from his accounts of feuds. He understood the mountaineer's feeling that it was his own business if he found it more profitable to market his corn crop as liquor instead of selling it as grain. The makers of the liquor tax laws were remote; but the revenue officers and constables who enforced the state and federal tax laws were at hand, and these became the physical targets for the moonshiners' hatred for what seemed to them an unfair tax. The cheapness of life, the ugly penalties of imprisonment and deprivation that went hand in hand with moonshining, the evils of illicit distilling—all these grew out of economic need. The deadpan delivery of these tales, both verse and prose, has heightened the impact of both the humor and the tragic incongruities that produce it.

Little Judd and Min Moore made moonshine to pay off a thousand-dollar mortgage on their farm at fifty cents a day in one Stuart poem. Judd was caught and sent to the *Pen*, and the mortgage holder slept with Min and deeded her the place. In the poem "Jim Long," the imprisoned moonshiner cried out:

> Why is it wrong for me to run a still?
> Now Uncle Sam's stool-pigeons sell and buy,
> And money is their God—their only cry!
> Sam Hix got fifty bucks to spy on me!
> Sam Hix, the dirty bastard, found my still.
> When I leave here—he is one man I kill!

More than one hill moonshiner felt that a *revenooer* hardly merited the status of a human being, and that spying local constables were no better. On his deathbed Mel Renfroe warned his erstwhile fellow moonshiner that he must face the consequences when the three dead revenuers that he had killed and buried in unmarked graves were resurrected; but Ceif Salyers remained untroubled, for the men were spying and "deserved what they got." In "Gallons or Bushels" another moonshiner, whose pretty daughter converted a disguised revenue officer to approving a *gallons instead of bushels* sale of the corn crop, threatened these hated spies, "We'd plant 'em where they'd never sprout." Yet another man shot an intruding constable and continued with his liquor run:

> The men next day saw old Bill stiff and cold.
> They said his mouth would make a trap for flies.
> One laughed and laughed and said: "God-damn his soul—
> He's snooping for the Devil—telling lies. . . ."
>
> He did not earn a place beneath the ground.
> Six feet of earth is far too much for him;
> We'll let hound dogs and piss-ants bury him.

Some of the moonshiners learned clever ways of dodging the revenuers and the law and succeeded in developing large-scale businesses. Among Stuart's characters in this category were Mose Winthrop, farmer, postmaster, and cattleman, as well as herb distiller, who had a *pull* with the law; he sometimes let one of his eleven moonshiners get into the county jail, but never let the law send them to the penitentiary. Another was Old Reliable Tid Fortner in *Foretaste of Glory*, a middleman between the moonshiners on his native Cave Branch and his lawyer, teacher, preacher, workingman, businessman customers in Blakesburg. During the roaring twenties he sometimes made one hundred dollars a gallon for the pure corn liquor; during the depression he cut his prices considerably, but the dollar bought more; after the repeal of the prohibition amendment he competed successfully with the sellers of government whisky. He built his business on quality:

. . . When his caravan of mules started toward Blakesburg with saddlebags across their backs, no one dared to bother this important load on its way to wet the dry gullets of important Blake County officials and Blakesburg businessmen.

Less adept at dodging the consequences of his brewing was Eif Cluggish in "Evidence Is High Proof," with his elaborate system of gunshot signals to warn his numerous *shiners* on different branches up different hollows. Keen Keat Battlestrife imitated Eif's signals and got enough evidence to serve as high proof: still and still-worm, gallon jugs of moonshine made from corn and sorghum, and nine *shiners*.

Disparaging references were made to Toodle Powell's *rotgut* in several Stuart stories, and Dennis Marcum's was said to have driven some men blind. Even Uglybird Skinner, seasoned drinker that he was, saw the Devil one night after drinking Dennis' product. By Stuart's count, the number of moonshiners around Greenwood, Blakesburg, or Greenupsburg (the place names are usually thinly disguised) ranged from sixty-eight peddlers of *sugar whisky* at two dollars a gallon during the early years of the Depression down to five or six after the repeal of Prohibition. In *Taps for Private Tussie* the number during World War II was set at "twenty-eight men that sold bootleg whisky in town on Saturdays, hoss-sale days, relief days and holidays."

The comic element, seldom absent from a Stuart story, runs to gross hyperbole in "Sylvania Is Dead," the story of a six-hundred-and-fifty-pound woman moonshiner who was "a mother to us all," who bought the hill man's corn crop and sold it back to him as pure, unadulterated moonshine. The revenuers caught her with a barrel of whisky, but were frustrated in their attempts at justice when they could not get her through the door of her own house. Her friends and customers who helped her husband bury her somewhat later on had to remove the chimney wall and lower the homemade coffin into the grave with five sets of plowlines. In *Daughter of the Legend* this story is moved into the Melungeon country of east Tennessee.

The dates of Stuart's stories of large-scale moonshining place the operations in an earlier period, but revenue officers are still capturing stills in the hill country in the late 1960s. Since legal whisky is readily available, continued moonshining indicates a continuing economic problem among the decreasing number of hill men who try to make a living on their farms.

The hill man has usually considered it his own business whether he made whisky or not—and equally his own business if he chose to get *white-muled, high as a Kentucky pine, full as a tick,* or drunk by any other name. Stuart has exploited this for humor in many stories, such as the following: the story of Temp and Fiddler Oll, the childless couple who drank their horse quart of moonshine and then fought in the streets, the man repeating "I love you, Temp," each time she knocked him down and helped him up so that she could knock him down again; Boliver Tussie's remarkable teeth biting holes in the galvanized pans and water buckets and holding on to the barbed-wire fence to keep his sons from taking him home in a borrowed jolt wagon when he was drunk; Uncle Jeff Hargis' invasion of private homes with his harmless repetition of "Woo-woo!" Very religious hill people, even some preachers, drank *Kentucky's Melancholy Dew* with a clear conscience. Stuart has rarely given straight-faced treatment to this truth of mountain life, but has exploited it for humor—the humor of Old Brother Peter Leadingham's visions, of the *funeralizing* for a Forty-Gallon

Baptist, of substituting urine for whisky in jugs left on the creek bank during church services, and of many more intimate portraits.

The adjustment from a ruggedly independent code to an acceptance of laws often considered unjust and administered by courts which inspired no confidence was a very difficult one for the hill man: "Where there's not any law to protect a man, there shouldn't be any to prosecute him." An early poem of Stuart's expressed the hill man's attitude:

> . . . "We've done no harm that we can see.
> We make our living from these sprouty hills.
> Our money goes to pay a lawyer's fee
> Because we operate our moonshine stills.
> We drink licker as we rake and plow.
> We make our living by sweat from our brow."

A code that could make a mother send out her sons at their mortal peril to *bushwhack* feuding enemies and that could approve shooting and secret burial of a man who interrupted operations at the moonshine still did not encourage men and women to grow squeamish at the hanging of a criminal. In at least two stories Stuart has achieved grim naturalistic comedy in his accounts of hangings as county-wide social occasions (hyperbole was surely at work in Grandpa's mention of a hanging every weekend for the entertainment of the Blake County population). "We used to go every Sunday of the world after church was out," said Grandpa in "Sunday Afternoon Hanging."

The biggest one he could remember was the hanging of five men for killing an old couple for money they were supposed to have had hidden in a teakettle. For this one, excursion boats ran, and a brass band was out. Each of the five men, in turn, stood on his coffin while the rope was secured around his neck; then the wagon was driven from under him, and his hands *glommed* at the wind while his face turned black and his tongue hung out. "He died strugglin' just like a possum struggles for breath after its neck has been broke under a mattock handle."

When the turn of the ringleader, Tim Sixeymore, came, his enormous bulk broke the hang-rope six times before his executioners could get a rope and a limb strong enough to hold him. His confession was as heavy with guilt as his body was on the hang-rope.

The hanging of Willard Bellstrase was dated 1903, an event that surpassed the Sizemore, Dimmer, Dillmore, Perkins, and Reeder *Hangin's*. School was dismissed and The Old Line Special ran an excursion train for the school children. Until Willard had slit a man's throat from ear to ear with a razor, Pa had defended him:

> "Eif, poor Willard's had a hard time . . . one of sixteen children. Used to fight like dogs and cats in the family . . . had to dig and hoe around on these old poor hills and try to help keep grub for the rest. Used to work him all day hitched to a plow."

By this time the condemned criminal had the dignity of a scaffold to stand on, and the trap door beneath him would open to let him swing by the neck. On his way to the scaffold he "scooted and *skived-up* the grass, cussed, hollered and prayed," while his family followed screaming, and his confession was merely a burst of defiant indignation.

Women fainted, men got *loaded to the gills* on moonshine whisky, young people courted, and children screamed while they waited for the doctor to feel Willard's *ticker* to make certain that he was a corpse.

Grandpa describes the decline of the hanging as a social occasion:

> Then a little later on they got to building a scaffold and just letting a body see their bodies before they dropped

down into a trap door and a sawdust bottom. They even put a cap over their face till people couldn't see their faces. Just kept a-gettin' it easier and easier until they didn't hang 'em at all. Got to having baseball games instead and then people got bad in these parts. Law got to be a joke. Something like it is now. Give 'em just as easy a death as possible, like the hot seat. They used to let 'em hang in Kentucky!

The hill man's gun was not always involved in defending moonshine stills, fighting feuds, and other such lawlessness. Hunting was one of the mountaineer's chief pleasures. "Pa allus said he'd rather be buried without an oak-board coffin as to hunt with a dirty gun," said Tarvin Bushman as he cleaned the family shotgun with meat rinds and a clean cloth. Rabbits, squirrels, birds, possums, coons, foxes—all presented their particular challenges to the hunter's skill and ingenuity. So detailed are Stuart's accounts of hunting, especially in the chapter "Opossums and Poetry" in *Beyond Dark Hills* and in the novel *Hie to the Hunters,* that a careful reader might well become a successful hunter by following Stuart's movement by movement instructions.

A good hunter looked for possums in valleys where wild grapes, persimmons, and pawpaws grew; he hunted on hilltops and in old fields on still, damp nights, and in valleys on windy nights. He had a well-trained dog with *a good nose,* a dog with strong forelegs, heavy shoulders and a thin body near his hips, a dog built for speed and power. He carried a lantern, a coffee sack, and a mattock, the mattock to dig the possum out of a hole or cut him from a hollow log if need be. He knew how to interpret his dog's barking from *cold-trailing* to *barking treed.* He learned to judge the possum's weight as he shook the tree, then gave the tree a little jerk that flipped the *sulled* possum from the treetop. Unless the possum happened to be fat on *simmons and pawpaws,* the hunter fattened him on buttermilk, apples, and other fruits to improve the flavor of his meat and the quality of his fur before he sold him. Stuart usually sold his possums to the Negroes for meat, got back the hides and prepared them for the fur market. Damp, quiet nights were best for tracking possums and coons.

Skunks, or polecats, whose hides were worth six or seven times as much as the possum hides, were best hunted in the rain to keep the smell down to a minimum. According to Stuart, the odor was offensive to the dog as well as to the hunter.

The hunter needed a quick eye and expert marksmanship for shooting the fast-moving rabbits, squirrels, and birds. Stuart had an eye for *rabbits a-setten:* he would see their ears around stumps, in leaf beds, and where the brims of tufted sod hung over ditches (he did not look for the tails, because they looked too much like *life-everlasting* with its gray leaves and tops), and could sometimes spot them from a distance of fifty feet. His father, however, thought it unsporting to shoot rabbits asleep and preferred to aim his long *flint-rock rifle* at the running rabbit after the dog had *jumped* him.

Big Eif Porter, whose death token came when *rabbits were ripe,* took his dogs to the *broom sage* and threw rocks and sticks into nearby thickets and brush piles to flush out the coveys of quail and the rabbits for his last supper on earth.

At Thanksgiving time Uncle Wash and his boys shot doves and woodcocks, fattened during the summer and fall on wheat, rye, and other grain around the barn, but Stuart and his father seldom killed birds, for they treasured them as flycatchers.

Tarvin Bushman hunted squirrels in the tall timber, for he knew that they liked to build their nests high up in hollow trees or in tall trees where wild grapevines were thick in the branches. He climbed stealthily up the bluff through the sprouts and looked upward from the spot where green hickory-nut shells were falling. He aimed at the squirrel's head as it jumped toward a nearby persimmon tree. Hunters of rabbits, squirrels, groundhogs, and other small animals usually aimed for the head so that they would not damage the meat or hide of the body. Some squirrel hunters, such as Uncle Kim Tussie and "Gunnery Higgins" in *Album of Destiny*, preferred to *bark* squirrels, not mutilating the animal at all.

Any time during the year, but especially on cool nights in April and October, hill men and boys liked to relax in the woods along the ridges, build a fire on the highest rock or peak in the vicinity, and listen to the barking of the fox as the dogs filled the night with *that purty hound dog music* (that to Op Akers' city daughter did not sound at all like music). The hill boy Sparkie said with some degree of exaggeration, "If I didn't git to fox hunt three or four nights a week from the beginnin' to the endin' of the year, I believe to my soul I'd die."

The foxhounds were trained for different functions in the chase. The *burn-out* dogs began fast and tired the fox, but also tired quickly themselves; the *cutter,* or *cuttin' dogs,* cheated by taking short cuts to get close behind the fox instead of taking the long circles around the mountain and along the ridges; *stay-dogs* that had the endurance to remain long in the chase sometimes crowded Old Hot Foot until he abandoned his usual ridge crossings and took *a nigh cut* down the hollow to escape them.

It was unthinkable to kill the fox during the *fox hunt,* for it would cause the hounds to slash and cripple one another fighting over the dead animal, and ruin the sport for months. In *The Good Spirit of Laurel Ridge* a runaway soldier who wrought havoc with the dogs and the hunters almost lost his life. The hill men do not eat the foxes, but they *trap* them for hides. Most popular of all hill hunting activities is this chase which is not really a hunt at all, in which the hounds never catch the fox and the hunters just sit and listen, talk, eat, or drink.

The hunter who was more interested in profit than in sport ran a trap line. The hill boy Sparkie and his town friend Did Hargis set a hundred steel traps over a distance of about twenty-five miles, in which they caught foxes, wildcats, minks, weasels, muskrats, possums, skunks, and coons. Sparkie knew that the traps must be set far enough away from *civil-i-zation* to reach wild country where the animals denned; he knew how to select spots where a hole worn slick between a split in the rock showed that animals were denning inside. Working with gloves to avoid leaving man scent, the boys scooped out enough earth to make the jaws of the trap even with the ground and covered them with dead leaves; they were careful to set the trap far enough back in the hole so that dogs would not be caught. A small sapling sharpened on one end served as the stake to hold the chain of the trap.

When running the trap line, the boys had to carry a gun to kill injured animals or dangerous ones. Sometimes only the animal's leg was left in the trap, showing that the animal was willing to buy his freedom dearly by gnawing off his own leg, perhaps only to die soon thereafter by some mountain stream. One trip to the traps yielded five polecats, twelve possums, two weasels, three rabbits, a coon, two foxes, and a wildcat.

The local color of fishing for fun and for sport along W-Hollow Creek, Tygart, and Big and Little Sandy rivers has received much less attention from Stuart than hunting; he has referred to it often enough, however, to show that it was a familiar part of hill life. With his small brother he dug *red-worm bait* around the hogpen and seined minnows with a coffee sack (or caught them on a pinhook with flies), for the easier-to-find *crawdads* did not make good bait.

Shan Powderjay helped Billie Auxier fish with worms for *mudcats* in Big Sandy. Old Alec caught fresh bass in W-Hollow Creek, using hook and line because he considered trot lines unsporting. Old Op whittled bows from cedar-wood and strung them with groundhog hide to shoot fish in the riffles of Little Sandy. He had to wrestle with a forty-pound *red hoss* that he had wounded with two arrows. Other hill men resorted to trapping fish, but Op did it only when he was too blind to see them. Stuart and a school friend fished from a raft on Tygart River near Carter Caves, but found the frogs and vicious turtles more numerous that summer than the fish.

Other hill pleasures have received varying degrees of attention in Stuart's writings. The county fair, an eagerly anticipated event in many hill communities, solved the problem of what to do with a cow-milking blue-tick pig: the manager of the fairgrounds bought him for $200 for a side-show attraction. Traveling carnivals (the fair usually included one) were considered wicked enough for some of the old-fashioned churches to *church* members who attended them, but they attracted many of the hill people when they came to the nearby towns. At one point during his boyhood Stuart replaced a carnival worker who had become angry and *hauled his freight*. He shared a tent with the fire-eater, who urged him to lay off the carnival women, who had *burnt* (with venereal disease) *nigh all the fellars* that had come in from the farms to work there. Stuart enjoyed his first night on duty at the Ferris wheel. The girls would scream and the boys would hold them more tightly; the boys would try to look up the girls' dresses above them, and the girls would spit down on them. He was asked to *haul his freight* for giving free rides to the pretty girls.

Another transitional pleasure, considered wicked by the Mountain Baptists, was going to the movies, or *picture shows*. During the convalescence from his heart attack, Stuart went to the theater in Greenup several times. He recalled in *The Year of My Rebirth* just how a country boy should behave at the small-town movies: he should supply himself well with candy bars, popcorn, peanuts, and soda pop before going in; keep his cap on, and if it made him more comfortable, put his feet on the back of the seat in front of him; laugh and talk, or walk out, if he became bored—but he knew to be quiet during the Saturday-night thrillers while the bullet-proof monster pursued beautiful blondes and terrorized whole towns; throw a paper bag with a few unpopped grains of corn or some peanut hulls, and hit an engrossed member of the audience during a particularly sentimental spot in the movie; and, in general, have fun.

Stuart has not overlooked pleasures of the home, school, and church. He has repeatedly referred to singing songs, listening to old-time fiddling, and telling tales around the fireside on winter evenings; to popping *cappers of corn* and making *popcorn and lassie balls* while chestnuts or *sweet 'taters* roasted in the ashes. He has written of women getting together to talk over their quilting on winter days, and of his mother's piecing quilts in the designs of wild flowers she saw and liked out in the woods. He has told of parents dressing children in their best to attend the Children's Day programs at the Sunday schools (in churches that approved of Sunday school), of parents' attending Christmas and end-of-the-term programs at the schoolhouse, of numerous home and church get-togethers. In *The Thread That Runs So True* he told of attending the Rock Creek Singing School, which differed from the usual *do-re-mi* and *fa-sol-la* singing schools in that the old and young people sang entirely by rote, taking their beginning note for each hymn and folk song from the leader's tuning fork.

Seeming inconsistencies in Stuart's panorama of hill pleasures and the code out of which they grew can be reconciled only by constant awareness on the part of his readers that Stuart has pictured a transitional period; the changes in his region have telescoped into one man's lifetime the cultural advancement of almost two hundred years in the world outside the hills.

By 1951 Stuart had written a story dealing humorously with the problem that television had presented to a church of the old-fashioned faith; at least one member was willing to be *churched* rather than forego his newfound pleasure. By 1955 Stuart's daughter had agitated for a TV set, and for the time being had been refused. Stuart, who recalled his own youthful appreciation of nature, feared that television would turn his daughter's attention away from books and the out-of-doors. He recalled that as a child he had never even heard of movies, radios, and phonographs and yet knew the fullness of life. Speaking on Jesse Stuart Day in Greenup in October, 1955, he expressed basic acceptance of change: "We cannot turn back. We have to live now, in the present, rejoice, dream, and lay plans for those tomorrows that may never come." This concept of dreaming, working, and never giving up has been characteristic of his people, the hill people.

Despite the suicides, the murders, the exodus of young people from his community, Stuart has portrayed hill men as basically pleasure-loving. His grandfather Hilton lived well past fourscore years and ten, and when asked which had been the best years of his life, replied: "Son, they have all been good years. But when I was the most powerful was between sixteen and seventy." Sometimes gross, boisterous, lusty, hard-hitting, danger-loving, they were also generous, sensitive, natural in their social relationships. From the sternest *figures of earth* to the oddlings like young Archie the artist in "Archie th' Oddlin'" and Jesse Stuart the poet, the hill people have shown in their pleasures the same ambivalence and leaning toward paradox that are everywhere apparent in the life of the region as a folk community.

CHAPTER FOUR

Kentucky Hill Schools

"Times has changed anymore. . . . Vote for me in
November and I'll make them like they used to be."
HEAD O' W-HOLLOW

In no other phase of hill life has Stuart pictured more
clearly the blighting effect of clinging to an outmoded tradition than in his accounts of Kentucky hill schools. He has
never failed to praise the heroic fortitude of the *figures of
earth* who carved a way of life out of the wilderness:

> . . . They raised their own tobacco and they used it; they
> made their own whiskey and they drank it. They carried
> firearms and used them in time of danger while they
> helped build America. What did they know about letters
> of the alphabet? . . . Why should they spend their time
> in a closed-up school-room, controlled by school authori-
> ties, and strive to learn to read secondhand life in books
> when they had firsthand life before them to live?

He has paid tribute to his father who could barely spell out
the words on tobacco *pokes*: "Earth was his book."

Stuart has understood why strong mountain boys and
girls went to the fields to sucker and worm tobacco, strip
and cut cane, hoe and cut corn instead of answering the call

of the school bell for *time of books*. He has understood, too, the resistance to change as a misguided attempt on the part of his people to achieve security in their lives. He has indeed been an *oddling*, however, in his militant and dynamic crusade for better schools.

Stuart stored up in the "album of his brain" vivid images of Kentucky rural schools from his varied experiences as a pupil at Plum Grove, a beginning teacher at Cane Creek (Lonesome Valley), and as Greenup County's youngest superintendent ever to hold office. Most of these impressions and the ideas born of them and of his experiences at Lincoln Memorial University, George Peabody College for Teachers, and Vanderbilt University have been recorded in his fiction and autobiography, notably in *The Thread That Runs So True*, selected by the *NEA Journal* as the most important book of 1949.

Nearly all of the rural schools were one-room and two-room barnlike structures in need of paint and repairs, badly located, inadequately ventilated in hot weather, and poorly heated by old-fashioned iron stoves in winter. Often the students or patrons helped the teacher cut stovewood to relieve the coal shortage. Sometimes a school had a *pie social* or some other fund-raising event to finance a paint or repair job. Parents sometimes helped cut away weeds and briar thickets from the schoolyard. The outdoor *privies* were usually smelly, full of flies, and marred by the usual latrinalia. Unless the teacher insisted upon it, not even lime was provided for improved sanitation. The water supply often had to be carried from a neighboring farm, and a single dipper served all the pupils. The teachers often had enough ingenuity to improve the appearance of the inside of the schoolroom with autumn leaves, wild flowers, and other native materials; but, as Thomas D. Clark has pointed out of another section of the state in an earlier day, Kentucky race horses were often housed better than the school children of Greenup County during the early 1930s.

Stuart has recalled repeatedly the stern discipline of his first Plum Grove teacher, whom he has called Professor Iron Hand. When a pupil misbehaved, one of the boys was sent up the cedar-pole ladder through the *scuddle hole* to the loft to get seasoned honey-locust and hickory switches, and the offender was soundly *whopped*. The strict disciplinarians of the old school believed in the saying *spare the rod and spile the child*; parents quoted it, but often disagreed with the teacher on the justification of his punishment. Stuart, for example, had to find another boardinghouse in Lonesome Valley after he had spanked the trustee's beautiful teenage daughter for spitting *ambeer* on the newly painted schoolhouse.

The Plum Grove schoolhouse had a platform, about one foot higher than the rest of the room, for the teacher's desk. Often such schoolhouses doubled as church houses, and not uncommonly the illiterate hill preachers ranted (from the same spot occupied on weekdays by the teacher) against the evils of *eddication*. A center aisle divided the *girls' side* from the *boys' side* (when Stuart broke this tradition at Lonesome Valley, parents accused him of running a *courting school*).

Stuart remembers that when he and his sister first walked to school along the three-mile-long path his father had mowed with a scythe, they wore homespun clothing, which his mother had made from wool raised, sheared, spun, carded, and woven on the little hill farm. Most of the boys were "overall-clad, barefooted with big rusty-looking feet"; and the girls wore cotton dresses and pigtails. The children carried their lunches, sometimes consisting of only corn bread and fried meat or baked potatoes, in little *dinner buckets*.

The pupils had no ready-made recreational facilities for recess periods and the lunch hour. The boys played *ante-over,* sending buckeyes over the schoolhouse, played *Round-town Ball* using homemade balls of twine wound around rags or a steely marble (it took a daring one to get it from among the tombstones in the churchyard, which Professor Iron Hand considered out of bounds), chased one another over the hills playing *Fox and Dog,* and played old-fashioned games such as *Jail, London Bridge, Among the Little White Daisies,* and *Needle's Eye* with the girls. It is possible that teachers with larger groups may have let the older boys roam over the hills when they were not reciting, as Anse Bushman tells Boliver Tussie that one of his teachers did: they fired hornets' nests, killed ground squirrels with rocks, and on snowy days tracked small animals to their dens.

The more ambitious pupils, using outmoded and tattered books, tried to spell down their classmates and get the most *headmarks;* they argued points of grammar with the teacher, and competed for honors in the arithmetic matches. Their hope of getting high up in *larnin'* beyond merely learning to *cipher,* read, *write fancy,* and *speak proper* lay along a path no less thorny than the Plum Grove playground before the wild-plum thicket was cut away; but school was an escape from picking beans, feeding hogs, and chopping wood, and to many of the children it seemed a wonderful place.

Often a school bully caused trouble for a teacher, and at some schools the older boys made a sadistic sport of running off the teacher, especially if their families were unfriendly toward him or the trustee who had appointed him. Stuart's oldest sister came home long before her term ended with shattered nerves and two blackened eyes. One of his former students was beaten up by a boy whose father had opposed her appointment. Stuart himself had to win a fist fight with a pupil before he could establish his authority at the Lonesome Valley School. It is possible that some teach-ers carried deadly weapons, as Anse Bushman says one of his teachers did when the older *scholars* gave him trouble.

The highly competitive nature of the hill boys did not al-ways follow constructive channels. Stuart remembers that every time he tried to do "some miraculous thing" such as jumping off the highest post, eating the most apples, being the toughest fighter, he got into trouble both at school and at home. "It happened that I was never the teacher's pet." His sister continually told on him: "Mom, Jesse got a whip-pin' today. He hit Bill Weaver with an apple core. He tore down the girls' playhouse. He got into Mrs. Collins' apples. He tore down a *doodle* of Mr. Wheeler's cane hay by run-ning and tumbling over it. He even said a bad word." Fight-ing among the pupils on the way to and from school was a major problem for rural teachers, and a hard one to settle because so often parents were involved in the fights.

When Jesse Stuart at seventeen unlocked the schoolhouse door at Lonesome Valley and let the school bell ring out over the cane fields, much in the situation was typical of Kentucky rural schools. The young teacher, chiefly self-educated, had fifty-four subjects to teach to pupils in eight grades, whose ages bore little relationship to their rank in school. He recalled later: ". . . I had ten-year-old pupils just starting to school. Nineteen-year-olds in the first grade. Fourteen-year-olds in the second grade. I had one twelve-year-old girl in the eighth grade."

As both teacher and superintendent, Stuart found, how-ever, that the hill children responded well to suggestions for which they were given sensible reasons, to beauty in their surroundings, to enthusiastic teaching that focused on the relationship between book learning and everyday life, and wholesome competition. At Lonesome Valley the pupils brought their own drinking cups, helped paint the schoolhouse, and took great pride in winning an arithmetic match with another school. Some hill pupils such as Tarvin Bushman who were *fast larners* were interested only in marrying and farming their rocky hills. Another boy, Jud Sparkie Sparks, who had given up school in the second grade, could not see in education enough to compensate for giving up *terbacker chawin', fox 'huntin'* at will, and emptying his revolver at the moon out of high good spirits; he, too, preferred to marry a hill girl who would be a *woman fer a livin'* and go on with the *corn and terbacker patchin'*. But there were those who needed only the prick of compulsory attendance and an interested teacher to motivate *book larnin'*: when the law forced Sid Tussie, Vittie's *woods colt*, to enter school, he thought that he had "just as well larn it all" while he was there, and he progressed from the primer to the fourth grade within a few months, much as Don Conway and Guy Hawkins had done at Lonesome Valley.

Early in his career as a teacher, Stuart realized that only through convincing demonstration in the laboratory of real life could he or anyone else get his people to change their attitudes and give their full support to promoting better schools. Stuart belonged to the generation of young hill people in his region who broke the isolation of the hill community. He knew of perhaps half a dozen others in his county who had college degrees at the time he received his from Lincoln Memorial University. He knew well the reasoning of the hill people about education: people such as Uncle Casper, who got as far as the eighth grade, got a teaching certificate, and *teached* fifty-nine years; like illiterate Uncle Radner, who thought schools a "big public expense for absolutely nothing" ; like Baptist Brother Tobbie, who considered a college education the road straight to Hell; like moonshiner Theopolis Pratt, who threatened with a rifle the first man to lift a shovel of dirt toward building Maxwell High School and upsetting the way of life there;

like trustee Ceif Anderson, who used the school as a means of gratifying his own petty aspirations to power politics; like his father, who reluctantly admitted that book learning was worth more to his son than corn bread and buttermilk: "You'll need it before you get through the world."

Others of the same generation, such as Grandpa Hilton (subject of many Stuart stories), were self-taught and acquired such a respect for knowledge that they urged their children and grandchildren to go to school and to become teachers that others might live more fully. Many could see at least the practical aspects of learning the three R's:

> They say that we are children of the night.
> My wife and me can't nuther read ner write—
> Though my son Paul—he's going off to school,
>
> When he grows up and learns a lot from books,
> I guess he'll be ashamed of my poor looks.
> But I want him to git some learning, see,
> So he can figure land and crops fer me.

Anse Bushman, who stayed in school long enough to learn how to cipher, read, and write before his class inadvertently burned down the schoolhouse and put an untimely end to their schooling, felt that the three R's had been a great help to him, but when education was given too much attention *books hurt the flesh.* He could figure land and crops and draw up an *ar-tickle.* Stuart's school patrons accepted gratefully and sometimes wonderingly the assistance from him and his pupils in surveying a field, in estimating how much dirt to remove for a well or a cellar, or how much a corncrib or wagon bed would hold—services based on simple arithmetic. Some hill people held the distorted concept that once a person had an education all he had to do to earn a livelihood was to go about with a pencil behind his ear: "I wanted to send Finn to school and make a big lawyer 'r doctor out'n him or a schoolteacher *so he could walk with a pencil behind his ear* and not have to cut the same sprouts from the same hill every year." Even Grandpa Tussie, who never would have thought of sending Sid to school if the attendance officer had not forced him to, was proud of the boy's achievements. Men who worked with Stuart's father on the railroad section were proud of their indirect connection with one so *high up in larnin'* as Jesse Stuart.

When difficulties arose in a rural school, Stuart found that the trouble often had its inception in the ignorance and prejudice of the parents; and he laid much of the blame at the door of the trustee system:

> Reports sent beyond this state that we didn't count our election votes until we had counted our dead, had good factual foundation. But many people believed this statement concerned county, state, and national elections between the two major political parties. It did concern them, but only in a minor degree as compared to these trustee elections. . . . It was a certain church group pitted against another church group. It was the "wets" against the "drys." It was feuding clan against feuding clan . . . it didn't matter which trustee was elected . . . the candidate he had defeated and his following . . . made life impossible for the teacher. . . .
>
> Guns were often brought into play at these elections. Men were killed and seriously wounded. . . . Scarcely ever was there a peaceful election.

Greenup County had 82 *deestricts*, each with three trustees, or 246 trustees. Trustees and would-be trustees came to Stuart during his superintendency with complaints against their rivals; a certain trustee had kissed the teacher before her pupils; a pupil had beaten up the teacher because the trustee who had appointed her was an enemy of his family; an enemy of the trustee who had appointed another teacher turned the *privy* over on the teacher. Stuart understood why the state had passed legislation in 1909 to make the county board of education a middle agency between the state office and the trustees, but not the passing of a law in 1931–1932 to raise the number of trustees from one to three for each district.

When Stuart struck the most bitter verbal blows of his better-schools crusade against the district trustee system, he was striking at an old and jealously guarded tradition of his folk, patterned after the old English hundreds (approximately a hundred pupils to a district). In Kentucky the county boards had been abolished in 1856 and restored in 1909 because the state found the system of dealing directly with the districts unwieldy. Major investigations by conscientious educators were made of the entire state education system in the late 1920s and early 1930s, one of the results of which was legislation in 1934–1935 that permitted county boards to eliminate the trustees. As recently as 1949, 17 of Kentucky's 120 counties still retained the system. Stuart's board members—even his most loyal friend on the board, a man who had gone free in a sensational murder trial and was quite unafraid of differing from group sentiment—sincerely voted against their superintendent's proposal to go on record as opposing the system. The board member who exploded into profane and indignant objections was probably expressing the general feeling of the rural people: "Well, I'll be goddamned, what else will you propose?" Another protested more mildly: ". . . I believe in the old way. It was good enough for me. It's good enough for the children of today. The trustee system is a wonderful thing. I was trustee for nine years." Stuart, for all his tribulations and rejections, had paved the way for his successor to be the first county superintendent in Kentucky to reduce the trustees to unofficial advisers. When the board in an adjoining county took a similar action, such all-out war resulted that the board was forced to go back to the old system.

On the part of both old and young, the attitude toward education seems to have given it a back seat to many things: farm work, funerals, marriage, among others. The parents would have held it against the teacher if he had not dismissed school for a neighborhood funeral, for it was a social occasion as well as a way of showing respect for the dead. With the coming of improved school facilities, better prepared teachers, the breakdown of the trustee system, and some degree of economic relief in the hills, it has become easier to enforce attendance laws during the period since World War II.

Aside from the transportation problem that made it impossible to transport Warnock students from the back of the county to the large county high schools, Greenup County High School students had many more advantages than the elementary rural pupils during the 1920s and 1930s. In 1929–1930 Stuart found that Warnock, on the Tygart River location of the Winston High School of his writings, was a delightful folk community. Immediately following his college graduation, he was sent there as the total faculty for a branch high school to teach all freshman subjects to the fourteen students interested in attending, even algebra and plane geometry, which he had never taken very seriously before. This variety of "comprehensive high school" challenged even this energetic graduate of the one-room country school who could recognize in his students the drive that had taken him through college. He began his duties by scything the small schoolyard and cutting the stubble, clearing away the wasp cones, birds' nests, and bats from the building that had served as a stable, a lodge hall, and then a barn. Almost immediately the fourteen strangely assorted looking students demonstrated unusual learning ability, creative imagination, and strong motivation. Stuart has repeatedly paid high tribute to these rural students whose resourcefulness and keen, receptive minds enabled some of them to win honors in state scholastic contests that year and to go on to high school and college in the face of almost insurmountable obstacles. For that year at least "all his geese were swans."

He has written a story "Charles" as a tribute to one of the poorest, homeliest, and most intelligent of these, a boy whose mother went insane and committed suicide horribly by wrapping herself in blankets and setting fire to them: ". . . I'm not a good teacher. . . . I just had the best timber that ever grew. . . . I have received advancement after advancement in schoolwork. I don't know what it is to fail. It is because of the immortal memory that I hold of one student—Charles." Stuart has told of walking seventeen miles across the hills to get books for these students and of getting lost in a snowstorm at night in sub-zero weather. He saved himself from freezing by pulling fodder shocks over him until daylight came. He tells how his little muleback cavalry rode to Greenup (Landsburgh) in almost equally bad weather to take the qualifying tests for the state competition, and took an easy victory over the town students.

Alert as the students were and high as their achievement was in scholarship, they found time for recreation. As far as Stuart's experience was concerned, the Warnock neighborhood was free from the petty rivalries found in so many hill communities. Stuart was entertained in his students' homes, their families having been conditioned to boarding the teacher in an earlier day. Almost every family had a self-taught musician who sang, played a banjo, fiddle, guitar, mandolin, or accordion; and several sometimes got together and played for hours at a time. Stuart went to the *workings* with his students; he went fox hunting with them, and taught them things he had learned about tracking game and preparing pelts for marketing; when the river froze over in winter, he skated and sleighed with them and helped them cut holes in the ice and gig fish; when the snow melted into sloppy mud, they played floor games such as darts, throwing bolts into a box, and *Fox and Goose* with homemade playing boards and colored grains of corn. The natural impulse of the educator whose zest for living equaled his interest in teaching made of every situation a teaching and learning situation in which work and play, freedom and responsibility went hand in hand; and these students, more accustomed to responsibility and with fewer distractions than town students, responded enthusiastically to his teaching.

Stuart credited the success of his contest-winning Winston freshmen with opening to him the opportunity to be principal of Greenup High School the following year. His writings of that year reflect the more pleasant aspects of the folk community influence chiefly through the eyes of a New York City girl who taught English on his faculty, the Helen Kirsten of *The Thread That Runs So True*. She told him one day: ". . . Poetry is in these people from your hills. Your hills, rivers, trees, log shacks, crying waters, wild flowers, and little fields of grain . . . have put this poetry in them . . . people talk with rhythm. Their language is poetry." She got on the school busses on Friday afternoons and spent weekends in the homes of her mountain students, attended the workings and parties, never mentioned the absence of bathrooms and screened windows and other inconveniences, and stimulated her students to write clear, image-making, rhythmic themes in their native speech, correcting only the gross errors and appreciating their gift for vivid and natural expression. The inbreeding that had so long perpetuated an older culture only a few miles out of the stream of American cultural and industrial progress had no place in Jesse Stuart's philosophy of education.

An interesting difference in values of the hill folk and the town people is pointed up by a detail of that year's experience that Stuart has never forgotten: a member of the board of education made an appointment with him to make a criticism of his appearance. Students had told their parents that he was dyeing his pants—the *dye* was ragweed stain from his four-mile walk across the hills from W-Hollow. He has written little in the satiric vein or otherwise on the hill man's adjustment to the conventions that the sophisticate expects of those who inhabit his social world, but he makes it clear that he considered many matters of school administration of more importance than the absence of ragweed dust on his trousers.

For the most part, this account of Kentucky hill schools has stressed the traditional elements that were part of the regional folk culture. Little in that tradition of hard farm work, illiteracy, feuding, and moonshining encouraged or qualified a hill boy or girl to pursue knowledge beyond the country school. "I heerd ye's a mighty stuck-up people since ye boys went to high school. Heerd y's eddicated and soft," remarked the Powderjay cousins of Shan and Finn, fictionized Stuarts. On the other side of the fence, Stuart has written of his and his sister's entrance into Greenup High School, "The other students didn't take to us very well." The Stuarts found themselves conspicuous because of their countrified clothes and ways, their lunches of cold corn bread and biscuits with meat and mustard between. They found that the Plum Grove School had not given them the background of subject matter that their classmates had received. "I hated them because I couldn't beat them and lead my class," Stuart said.

Like other hill students since Jesse Stuart's school days, he adjusted rather quickly to high school. By his senior year he tied for first-place scholastic honors, played on the first-string football team, attended parties with the town students, and took the town boys into the hills on hunting trips. Nine years later, when he returned as principal of the school, he found that the gulf between rural and town students had lessened considerably. The town students still laughed at the ungainly spectacle of Burton Waters, the "Charles" of Stuart's story of that title; but once they recognized the keen perception of his remarkable mind, they admired him. The mutually beneficial effects of sharing experiences among students of different backgrounds and with different ideas became apparent to Stuart and influenced others through him from his earliest teaching.

When a few ambitious young hill people such as the Stuarts began walking out of the remote hollows and across the hills to the county-seat high school, a significant new influence began to operate in hill life: the awareness of differences was the beginning of leveling. Parents, neighbors, younger brothers and sisters began to hear and think about things from outside the hills. As the Powderjay cousins' remark suggested, the surface changes in clothing, manners, personal habits, and manner of speaking sometimes evoked sarcasm and scorn from the illiterate stay-at-homes. These and deeper changes of attitudes, ideals, and ambitions, however, increasingly stimulated the younger boys and girls to go forth and prove that they could do as well as their relatives and neighbors. As the practical values of education, to say nothing of the aesthetic values, became more and more evident, the hill people began to undergo a change of attitude toward education. The early influence of these young hill people who blazed the trail toward high-school and college education can hardly be overestimated; but the conditioning process necessary to gain the fullest possible support of the voting population for equal opportunities in the rural and urban sections is still at work in Kentucky, as in certain other parts of the country.

If the hill background did little to encourage high-school attendance, it did much less to suggest to boys and girls that college or university study was possible and desirable for them. When Jesse Stuart went away to college only one relative on either side of his family had preceded him, his cousin Everett Hilton on his mother's side. When he returned to Greenup County in 1929 with a Bachelor of Arts degree from Lincoln Memorial University, he was one of perhaps half-a-dozen native-born persons in the entire county to have a college degree. Physical stamina, natural intelligence, and will power as *strong as the tough-butted white oaks* of his region had enabled Stuart to finance his education entirely through his own efforts. As in high school, Stuart had adjusted well, supported himself, participated in school activities, and maintained an honor average in his academic work.

After Stuart had been appointed to the principalship of Greenup High School, he went to George Peabody College for Teachers at Nashville in the hope of learning ways of improving the instruction and management of the school; and many of the ideas that shocked his board members and former friends into profane objections were suggested or influenced by his summers of study and his consultations with faculty members there.

Jesse Stuart's interests in teaching and writing alternated and coincided. Because of the low salary at Greenup High School, he decided to spend his share of the profit from the family tobacco crop on a year at Vanderbilt University. He studied English under Donald Davidson, Edwin Mims, John Crowe Ransom, Robert Penn Warren, and others who were famous writers as well as teachers. Many snags beset his course that year: the tobacco crop failed, leaving him penniless; working for eleven meals a week and his room in one of the dormitories interfered with his study; his disinclination and lack of training for documented research created problems even before his arduously written thesis burned in the dormitory fire that also left him jobless; until toward the end of his year at Vanderbilt the great men on the faculty who had attracted the young writer-educator took little notice of Stuart. Then Donald Davidson, especially, began to recognize his ability; and Dr. Mims (who nevertheless left his course grade in Victorian Literature "Incomplete") was convinced that writing genius lay back of the autobiography Stuart gave him instead of a term paper, the work that was to be published as *Beyond Dark Hills.*

The ambivalence of Stuart's feelings about his year at Vanderbilt has shown clearly in his published work. He left without a degree, but with contacts that Dr. Davidson and Dr. Warren had made for him with New York publishers and prominent magazine editors, and with the stimulation of their interest in his poetry and prose. Dr. Davidson particularly had talked with Stuart encouragingly and appreciatively. "He told me to go back and write of my people in Appalachia as the Scots, Irish, and English have written of their countries, or segments of their countries—like Thomas Hardy in the Heath Country and Yeats in Ireland," Stuart says of Davidson. At the end of the year, as Stuart hitchhiked his way on a dynamite truck to go home and once more hoe corn in W-Hollow, his thoughts ran thus:

> Wasn't Vanderbilt University a great school after all! Wasn't it strange to be in school where teachers and students were writing books! Didn't they smoke in class at Vanderbilt. . . . And if you got stewed . . . didn't he [the University Law] take you to the dormitory and put you to bed and tell you what a good man your father was when he came to this university? . . .
>
> Wasn't one of the ministerial students one of the best poker players in the University? . . . Didn't many of the professors keep jugs of corn licker made in the Tennessee hills in their homes because they couldn't get legalized whiskey? . . . And when I asked Doctor Mims if I could get a degree without writing a thesis didn't he refer me to

the dry pages of the catalogue and ask me to read for myself, and that was that. Vanderbilt University, upon a little hill, overlooking the city, unmolested throughout the years, going on quietly and watching the students come and go.

The indirect and ultimate effects of this year that Stuart spent at Vanderbilt University upon his county superintendency and his teaching during four years at Maxwell High School that followed—upon the students and people of the community, and upon education in the entire Greenup County area—can hardly be calculated.

Stuart's life has known little monotony, and has been notable for contrasts. The year after his term at Vanderbilt he served as Kentucky's youngest county superintendent of schools in one of the state's largest counties, where the school system had become "a broken down horse." In that depression and transitional year of 1932–1933, Stuart worked for the minimum salary allowed in the state. The only well-to-do district in the county had withdrawn from the county system and was demanding tuition from the rural students. The treasury was bankrupt, and the board of education could not get credit. Money was not available for teachers' salaries beyond the third month, and old debts could not be paid. Corrupt practices of preceding years created additional problems. Stuart and his board had to cope with thirty-two lawsuits during the year. Stuart's account of this year as one of Kentucky's and America's *fightingest* educators shows it to have been the stormiest of his career. As a one-man representative of ideas promoted by one of the most respected and progressive teacher-training institutions in the South, Stuart found himself with a board of education firmly grounded in such ancient traditions as the trustee system, shackled further by their concern over personal and family feuds, and at odds among themselves. Headstrong in his practical idealism, Stuart plunged headlong into a program of budget revision, bus transportation of students to the western end of the county as cheaper than paying tuition for them at Greenup, attempts to resolve lawsuits, and attempts to interest the state leaders as well as the local ones in taking reform measures in this "mother of all the professions."

A vivid picture of ignorance, ineptitude, inequalities and inadequacies, and downright corruption in the school system emerged from Stuart's writings of that year. Stuart's youth and exuberance added salt to the wounds he had inflicted by striking with deadly intent at so many set ideas and outmoded practices in local school administration. Far from viewing Jesse Stuart as a fountainhead of constructive ideas, they looked upon him as a dangerously erupting volcano that could only spread destruction in its path: even former friends turned against him as a born troublemaker who was out to wreck the school system. Yet he was able to plant many seeds that year that were to bear fruit later when state legislation helped to bring about reforms to benefit both students and teachers.

Closely related to Stuart's denunciation of the trustee system was his militant advocacy of a county unit plan of school administration to eliminate some of the inequalities of opportunity for pupils and the incredible variation in working conditions and salaries for teachers. It was possible under the dual system for the superintendent of an independent district to earn a larger salary than that of the state superintendent. Consolidation of schools could equalize the wealth of the county instead of concentrating its benefits in the four independent districts, particularly the town of Greenup. Industrial organizations, exploiting the wealth and labor of the rural sections, tended to patronize the town schools where the greatest influence lay toward industrial tax legislation. During the year 1932–1933 the average monthly salary for a rural teacher in Greenup County was

$65 for a seven-month term, the maximum of $79.80 going to teachers with college degrees and maximum experience; salaries in the independent districts were often more than double the county ones. One year the salary of the superintendent of one of the independent districts was $4,200 for the year, $200 more than that of the state superintendent. In a state such as Kentucky that was predominantly rural Stuart could see this dual system only as the tail wagging the dog.

Not only the low salaries and poor teaching conditions but also the absence of tenure and pension laws kept Stuart's typewriter busy during this eye-opening year as county superintendent of schools. One rural teacher told him that he prayed daily for good health so that he could continue teaching and for a sudden death when he could no longer teach so that he could avoid the disgrace and squalor of a mountain poorhouse. Another, who had a college degree earned slowly over many years, had been pushed aside because of advancing age and was grateful for a mountaintop school that was hardly accessible for younger persons: "I have to teach school, Mr. Stuart," she told her superintendent during his county-wide visitation of schools. "I've taught all my life and I've never been able to put anything away for a rainy day." Stuart could not get his articles into print in the local publications, and at that time he did not consider national publications. Even his father thought that he had "bumfuzzled the superintendent's job."

"We will all be defeated when we run again, if we support you," one of Stuart's board members said of reappointing him as superintendent. "That doesn't matter. . . . You've stood by this county; there are a few honest men in the world, and you are one." But Stuart did not permit them to make that last-ditch stand for him; instead, he asked for and received the principalship of the west-end high school where he could pursue his goals by his own methods more quietly. He had worked Siberian salt-mine hours. He had moved in an atmosphere that bristled with antagonism and guns. He had fought with the single-minded idealism of youth against a complex structure of personal greed and grievances, inflexibility of mind hardened by long-held concepts, and the tendency of the entire commonwealth from its beginnings to look upon education as a private matter rather than as a public responsibility.

By this time, Jesse Stuart had laid a number of bricks to pave the way for the revolution in hill education that was to come during the next two decades, as improved transportation and communication brought sweeping changes into all phases of hill life.

The "large consolidated schoolhouses, with spacious playgrounds, big athletic fields, large libraries, and big gymnasiums" have largely replaced the barnlike structures of the past as Stuart dreamed that they would. Bus transportation has brought elementary and secondary education within reach of pupils from the most remote hills and hollows. By 1935–1936 the county unit was the usual system of administration. Soon thereafter the Teachers Tenure Law and the Teachers Retirement Law improved the lot of Kentucky teachers. But in spite of substantial gains, with some salaries nearly doubled between the years 1960 and 1965, Kentucky still lags far behind the nation's average. As Stuart noted in the 1940s, Kentucky's excellent teacher-training institutions in the 1960s are still preparing teachers to work for somewhat more than *death-colored wages* in other states. The fact that Kentucky is predominantly rural and that it has undergone less change in the character of its population during the industrial revolutions than many neighboring states accounts to some extent for the difficulty of supporting an excellent program of public instruction. The fact also remains, however, that the people of Kentucky need to "feel more deeply the need for schools."

Following his year as one of the hardest-working and least-appreciated school administrators ever to take office in any state, Stuart gave up temporarily his struggle with finances and political intrigues and went home once more to hoe corn in W-Hollow. The next year he began a four-year career at McKell (Maxwell) High School in a beautiful valley setting, which was to be one of his happiest periods as an educator. In this, the most modern high school in the county, to which a wealthy Ohio physician had contributed munificently, with a relatively well-trained faculty of twelve college graduates that he had chosen, in a community that was conditioned to support education, he was able to try out many of his favorite theories and help many capable young people to attend college and prepare for the teaching profession. Out of this experience came not only one of the most thought-provoking sections of *The Thread*, but such short stories as "Split Cherry Tree," "Wild Plums," "Eustacia," "Last Method," "Teacher to Fit the Schedule," "Little Brier," and others. His experience there was interesting for his successful experiments with adult education, use of student help in as many phases of schoolwork as possible, and in general application of his philosophy that students with ideas are "like young streams without channels" and that the teacher's responsibility is to "direct each channel on its natural course" and work sympathetically with all students of varying interests, ages, and abilities, trying always to adapt the teaching to the need of a developing human being.

Although McKell High School was hardly a folk community, it drew students from the high mountains above the Tygart Valley, and certain incidents in Stuart's experience there reflect the folk traditions and the folk psychology of the Kentucky hills. One of his best students, Eustacia Pratt, was descended from the founder of the community, a Revolutionary War hero; her father, who had become a moonshiner and a murderer, was saved from the penitentiary only by his own sudden death—the man mentioned earlier who had fought education and threatened with a rifle the first man to lift a spade of dirt to build the high school. Stuart wrote a story about her, and gave her the money for her first year's expenses at Berea College, asking that she repay him by giving the same amount to her sister when she was ready for college. When New England philanthropist Henry Lee Shattuck, impressed by Stuart's fourth book, his autobiography *Beyond Dark Hills*, asked Stuart to recommend a student to be put through college at his expense, Stuart sent detailed accounts of three, and the wealthy man sent all of them (each paid one-fourth and enabled another to go), and arranged for a friend of his to send another. These included a hill boy poet-athlete-scholar who wrote in his science notebook poetry that captured the beauty of his hills, Lyttle Brier; two sons of a rural teacher who never could have sent them on his salary; and two girls who became teachers—"they were acorns dropped into a pool."

Those young hill people, like the Stuarts who were eager enough for a college education to get through in spite of poverty, radically different social background, and inadequate academic knowledge, often changed a great deal in their attitudes and ideas as well as in their outward appearance and conduct: "I could see that college had changed him," Stuart said of his younger brother. "He wore his clothes better. He was careful about choosing words when he spoke. He looked cleaner and his face looked keen and bright. . . . The dry, hard seed that was James Stuart was bursting into a very reticent masculine flower." And he has seen such transformations in many of his former students who likewise have surmounted the obstacles to getting a college education. His personal influence and attention to helping deserving students to get scholarships have been extensive.

Stuart enthusiastically overrode faculty opposition at McKell High School, and opened all classes to interested adults of all ages, especially to rural teachers who had not completed high school. "You couldn't tell the faculty from the students," he recalls. Soon after the publication of *The Thread That Runs So True* (1949), the University of Kentucky, of which H. L. Donovan was then president, greatly expanded Kentucky's adult-education offerings through the services of the university. Adult programs on all levels of education have proliferated throughout America since Stuart's pioneering efforts in Greenup County. The door has opened a little wider there for the people of Appalachia to enter today's world with dignity and hope. Yet in this seventh decade of the twentieth century Stuart's region and Appalachian America in general still lag in educational opportunities for both adults and children.

After four years at McKell High School, Stuart spent fourteen months traveling in Europe and the British Isles on a Guggenheim Fellowship, everywhere seeking to satisfy his insatiable desire to learn more and better methods of educating youth. Significant differences that he noted between the United States system of education and that of most of the countries that he visited included both favorable and unfavorable points of comparison and contrast. Teachers unquestionably had higher social and economic status in relation to the members of other professions outside the United States than in most of the states of the Union. On the other hand, the basic philosophy of a democratic education held in the United States seemed to Stuart superior to the educational philosophy and practice of most of the countries that he visited during 1937–1938.

He returned to Greenup to learn that new officials had replaced those who granted his leave of absence and he had no job. He accepted a position as teacher of remedial English across the river in Portsmouth, Ohio, and renewed his fight for reforms in the school system of Greenup County and Kentucky. He was alarmed by the infringements upon individual freedom that he had seen in so many countries of Europe, and tormented by the possibility that a continuation of such fascistic practices as those he could see at work in his native county might prove false the general feeling that "it couldn't happen here." From July to November he published his own newspaper, with a circulation increasing from 200 to 800 (he had not secured a permit to send it through the mails, which would surely have increased its circulation). He struck hard with facts that he could prove at the corrupt political methods that had put the current school administration in power and the corrupt or at best questionable actions its members had taken in the matter of employing, firing, retiring, and assigning teachers; and other areas of action that he considered threats to the freedom of his people. "The fight ranged from Washington, D.C., to Frankfort, Kentucky, to Mountain View, the farthest outpost rural school in Greenwood County." This hardfought battle with words almost cost Stuart his life. He was attacked from behind in a Greenup drugstore with a blackjack, and survived two blows that the examining physician thought might easily have killed a man. In 1939 Stuart gave up full-time teaching to become a lecturer, free-lance writer, and W-Hollow farmer; but he did not give up his interest in education and his fight for better teachers, improved teacher welfare, and the kind of schools he has believed in. He has lectured, assisted with workshops, and taught as a guest professor from coast to coast.

In 1956 Jesse Stuart, still convalescing from his almost fatal heart attack of 1954, returned as principal to his beloved McKell High School, challenged by the chaotic state of affairs reported there. An autobiographical novel, *Mr. Gallion's School* (1967), tells the story of that year. In this novel, Stuart has demonstrated his genuine faith in youth to accept meaningful responsibilities and to develop into confident and productive men and women.

During Stuart's eighteen-year absence from the school (here called Kensington High School), political compromise, poor teaching conditions, and community apathy had driven away most of the faculty and very nearly destroyed the school. Affluence and parental permissiveness had produced a restless new generation of "rebels without a cause." Gambling, hot-rodding, stealing, "skipping" school, destruction of property were all symptoms, he believed, of youthful confusion. Youth, Stuart believes, needs the security of a stable school organization administered by responsible and imaginative adults. Suspending or expelling confused or apathetic students he sees as an abdication of adult responsibility. *Involvement* is his guiding principle.

George Gallion went to work with the energy and confidence so characteristic of Jesse Stuart. He filled out his faculty with student teachers, organized the honor students into clean-up and repair crews (work should be a reward, never a punishment). He co-operated with his other faculty members in getting students in the band, the school farm activities, athletics, and all manner of scholastic competitions. He was not shocked or dismayed by obscenity, profanity, or insubordination; neither did he tolerate offensive behavior. As his school became more orderly, honor and pride supplanted hostility and tension. He understood youth's natural distrust of the parent generation; he had no quarrel with youth that was not a "lover's quarrel." He saw the school as the symbolic citadel of modern culture, "where products are shaped to change the world." His anger and frustration turned the focus again and again on the parent generation, who alone can provide the guidance youth does not know it needs, but without which it cannot develop its potential for achievement or happiness.

The book is a testament of faith in American youth, of

trust in American democracy, of acceptance of the human condition in the confused twentieth century world. The voice is less youthfully bold, but no less positive. The key phrases are not those of the generation coming of age in the 1960s—"amount to something," "love your country," "stand up and be counted," but the love of life which never falters comes through to old and young alike. To live well, in George Gallion—Jesse Stuart terms, is to savor the struggle. Stuart's earlier and more exuberant optimism has matured into a sober and realistic acceptance of violence and error as essential in human experience. This recognition of the lessons of history gives a new dimension to his humanistic certainties. As Thoreau suggested, he builds his castles in the air where they belong, and then tries vigorously to put foundations under them.

"I'm not much of a fighter until I have to fight," Stuart told Guy Hawkins, the school bully whom he defeated in a fist fight at Lonesome Valley when he was seventeen. In most areas of hill life, Stuart expresses a certain nostalgia for the traditional customs and lore of a bygone day, but not in his writings of Kentucky hill schools. He has fought with the indomitable spirit of his ancestors in his efforts to transform the sketchy *book larnin'* of the past into a modern and effective education for democratic American citizenship. *The needle's eye,* an effective system of public instruction, should supply *the thread that runs so true*—the kind of education that combines work and play, freedom and responsibility in the combination indispensable for the perpetuation of democracy in American life. He has recognized the need to gear the curriculum and activities of the schools to include special services for the gifted and the retarded students as well as for the normal ones; he has promoted adult-educational programs; and he has ever seen the only avenue of escape from the darker aspects of mountain life in the kind of education that draws upon all the resources of schools, communities, and human beings for fuller and more productive living.

"We educate our people or we perish . . ." is the strong motivating idea behind his lifelong crusade. On the tablet erected in the Greenup courthouse square in October, 1955, are the words: "Poet-Novelist-Educator"—and he takes great pride in the title "Educator."

CHAPTER FIVE

The Hill Man's Work

This man can use a cutter plow and axe,
A mattock, spade, pitch-fork and scythe and hoe—
This pioneer left over from the long ago. . . .

MAN WITH A BULL-TONGUE PLOW

As Stuart pictures the hill man, and as he actually was during the early twentieth century, he was first and foremost a farmer. From time to time during the evolution and decline of the community, *public works* offered occasional employment. Such employment accompanied the exploitation of hill resources with outside capital by companies relatively uninterested in the effects of their activities on the hill people. The hill men who worked in the sawmills, coal mines, and steel mills, on road construction or on the railroad section, usually considered the jobs an emergency measure. Even when the work continued over long periods of time, most of the men, with the help of their families, tried to keep their farms going. Some who sold their rocky acres for a pittance (Stuart has one character set the figure at twenty-five cents an acre for mineral rights) were dissatisfied with the new life but lacked the wherewithal to buy more land and return to farming. Whether the hill man devoted himself exclusively to farming, to a job away from the farm, or divided his time between the two, he worked strenuously and took grave risks.

Hardly any phase of farm work has been omitted from Stuart's writings. He tells of the little jobs as well as the big ones: cutting firewood and building the fire (starting it with rich pine *kindling*); feeding the livestock, cleaning and rebedding their stalls, currying and brushing the mules and horses; milking; cleaning out the sprouts and briars from the fence rows; caring for newborn, runty, or sick farm animals; spreading lime on the pastures and the barnyard manure on the croplands; building and repairing barbed-wire fences; checking the water holes in the pastures. The old squatter Alec did a good deal of the odd-jobs type of work commonly called *gin-work:*

> . . . He had cut dead trees near the fence so they wouldn't fall in a windstorm and smash it and let the cattle out. Dead trees near the water holes had been cut. Alec had taken care to see that the cattle wouldn't be in danger of an old tree falling on them when they went for water.

Other recurring jobs were sharpening tools and occasionally putting new handles in them; repairing harnesses; greasing and repairing wagons, disk harrows, plows; repairing leaky roofs and replacing rotten porch boards; filling in holes burrowed under fences or into the chicken house—the farmer's work was never done.

Building fences involved a briar scythe to cut the path for the fence; an ax, a maul, a wedge, and a crosscut saw to cut the posts from dead trees; a sharp, strong posthole digger that would penetrate the shale or even sand rock (sometimes a *spud* was used to dig through the rock); a *mattock* and a *grubbing hoe* to clear the sprouts; a *sledge* to haul the posts and equipment; *wire stretchers, pliers, hatchet, staples,* and *barbed wire.* These four- and five-strand barbed-wire fences rusted and were in continual need of repairs; the rusty wire would break and wrap around the men, so that they needed a bottle of iodine or turpentine along when they worked on fences.

The big jobs on the farm were clearing and preparing the land for planting, hoeing and plowing the fields to *make the crop,* harvesting and marketing or storing the crops in the fall. Such seasonal work as hog killing, molasses making, apple-butter stirs sometimes required outside help. At all times, except in winter, every member of the family helped with the work. Even a small child could carry water to the fields. "We all worked hard because existence in the hills compels whole families to work hard," wrote Stuart. Of himself: "I was introduced to the ax and sprouting hoe at six, the plow at eleven."

The preparation of the cropland began early in the spring. Often it was necessary to clear the land by cutting the timber, digging out the sprouts, forking them into wind-rows, and burning the brush heaps. Unlike many of his neighbors, Stuart's father tried to avoid having his land burned over, which he believed damaged the *leaf-rot* loam of rich new ground and caused erosion. Those who burned the new ground chose a time when the wind was still and divided the family into two groups—one to fire uphill on one side of the ridge, and one on the other so that the fires would meet and not spread. The wild game tried to escape, but terrapins, frogs, lizards, young possums, rabbits, and even birds as well as the hated snakes burned. After the main fire had burned out, someone went in to dig out stumps, cut saplings, and *chunk the brands* until all snags, stumps, and loose poles had burned, leaving the ground smooth enough for the plow.

Whether or not the farmer burned off the ground, his *bush blades, briar scythes, mattocks, saws, sprouting hoes, axes,* and *pitchforks* were likely to go into action in late

March or early April—as soon as the ground had thawed from the winter snows. The big *one-eyed hoe* was the *darb* for cutting sprouts—the little sourwood sprouts which snapped off, the tougher sassafras sprouts, and the saw briars, which were toughest of all. Old Op Akers, a champion sprout cutter, would attack a tangle of wild grapevines, making a thicket around the trees by cutting from the outer rim of the circle in enough places to make the brush fall neatly piled. In sprout cutting, corn hoeing, almost any type of farm work, a spirit of competition spurred the men on.

In all seasons the farmer's day began about four o'clock, an hour that impressed outlanders. *Early to bed and early to rise makes a man healthy, wealthy, and wise:* the hill man often quoted the old proverb which seemed rather incongruous in the light of his low economic status.

Walking between the handles of a mule-drawn or horse-drawn *bull-tongue* or *root-cutter plow,* the farmer broke up the root-filled rocky soil; he then harrowed it to break the larger clods before he *laid the ground off* in furrows. Sometimes new ground needed only to be *double-furrowed* for planting. When the ground was roughest, oxen were used to pull the plow; then sure-footed mountain mules; next horses; and now tractors. "A body's got to cuss when a plow jabs his ribs or punches him in the belly," says Pa in "One of God's Oddlings," and he goes on to tell of attending a funeral of a man fatally hurt when a plow kicked him in the *touchy parts.* Even so, Stuart seems to feel a certain regret at the passing of the Kentucky mule as the machine age has reached into the hills.

Corn and potatoes were among the first crops to be planted, as they provided basic foods. The Stuarts planted potatoes on Good Friday, and soon thereafter planted in the garden patch the peas, beets, radishes, carrots, and lettuce. Stuart remembers that meals were meager in years when the corn and potato crops both failed. He pictures Subrinea Tussie in *Trees of Heaven* planting the corn methodically, three grains in a hill with a long step and a short step between the hills, and another person following her closely to cover the grains immediately, before the crows and other birds could eat the seeds. Pumpkin seeds were planted through the corn and around stumps; and cornfield (pole) beans were planted in some of the fields of corn. If the farmer *got a season*, the *awfullest corn came poppin' out'n the ground;* and soon it was *foul* with *a hurricane of weeds*. To make the crop, the whole family *humped to it* and *bore down on their hoe handles* to *murder the weeds*. When the crop was *out of the first weeds* and the field *so clean that a crow would have to carry his grub across it*, the family could turn their attention elsewhere until time for the final cultivating which would *lay the crop by*. The corn hoers would each try to *hold the lead row* so that the person hoeing the row above him could not *smear his balk* and make the hoeing harder for him, especially on days when the sun was *hot as a roasted 'tater*. *It takes a strong will and a weak mind to make a crop in the hills*, the hill farmers would sometimes say; but *the smell of cornfields gets in your craw*.

Unless drought *burnt up the crop alive* and dwarfed it to *bumblebee corn* or the *fallen weather* amounted to a cloudburst that washed the topsoil into ditches, the farmer could hope for a *gollywhopper* of a crop—enough to provide bread for the family and feed for the stock and chickens. A cold, wet season, of course, could cause the seed to rot in the ground, and cutworms or *crawdads* could destroy crops planted in the creek *bottoms*. The hill farmer had to be philosophical, for he recognized "the way of hill life—feast today and famine tomorrow."

If frost hit the corn, the fodder had to be *railroaded* at once to make the feed safe for the cattle. If not, a *corn-*

shucking or a *fodder-pulling* might accompany or precede
the harvesting of the crop. Sparkie in *Hie to the Hunters*
instructed the town boy Did Hargis in the details of harvesting the corn crop. First he had to learn to harness the
mules and hitch them to the sled or plow: he had to be
careful to get the *near mule* on the *near side* and the *off
mule* on the *off side* if he expected the mules to pull as a
team; he learned how to put on the padded *collars,* place
the *britchen* across their backs, fasten the *hame strings,*
and buckle the *bellybands;* he learned to use the *clevis* and
open links to secure the *doubletree* to the *singletrees* and
the *singletrees* to the *trace chains;* he watched carefully to
avoid having the *trace chains* come loose and *swarp* the
mules on the legs. When all the corn had been hauled on
the sled to the barn, and the corn nubbins were in the bins,
it was time to shock the fodder. Three persons could work
well as a team: one cut the fodder, another shocked it, and
a third plowed under the remaining stubble. The cut fodder
was pulled into large shocks which were tied with wild
grapevines or something equally strong.

Anse and Tarvin Bushman did the work a little differ-
ently: they walked upon a slope where the buff-colored fodder blades rattled in the autumn wind and bent four corn-
stalks across the balk and looped their tops together every
twelve hills; they cut four rows of corn through the field on
each side and placed the stalks around these *riders;* then
they tied two bands around the shocks. They worked all
night while the fodder was damp with dew and easy to
handle.

The Bushmans dug their potatoes with a pitchfork to
avoid bruising them, and drove the mules and sled between
the rows to load the potatoes into the straw-lined sled bed.
Into the bin went enough for the winter's food supply;
holed up in a mound of dirt with a ditch around it to drain
off water were the seed potatoes and spring food supply

(almost surely Fronnie Bushman *graveled* a few potatoes for table use before the crop was made).

The tobacco crop was the money crop in Stuart's region, as he has indicated in several stories. In *Trees of Heaven* and *Hie to the Hunters* he has given detailed and realistic accounts of tobacco farming from the making of the plant bed to the marketing of the crop. The soil had to be wet to receive the rank, sticky, smelly plants in early May. The young plants had to be kept free from weeds, had to have the suckers removed as they appeared, and the big green tobacco worms pulled in two. The men had to take their to-bacco knives to the patch at just the right time, slit the stalks toward the root, hack them off, and put four or five on a stick, put the sticks in the ground to dry until they could bring around the sled and haul them to the open to-bacco barn. There they were hung with the tips downward from tier poles. The men's clothing became sticky with the green tobacco glue. A rainy season in the fall put the to-bacco *in case.* When the curing tobacco was "soft and pli-able as sun-wilted sassafras leaves in July," it was ready to come down off the tier poles for *stripping* off the leaves, grading them, and tying them in *hands,* ready for the market. The work of stripping had to be done before the tobacco dried out, or the farmer would have to wait for an-other tobacco *season.*

> "Terbacker is damn hard stuff to raise and make money out'n," says Pa, "all I ever try to make out'n it is tax money. You know it's a little money crop. Raise enough corn to do us and other truck and sell the terbacker. Sow beds for plants when the March snow is on the hill. Strip it at damp spells in winter time. Terbacker is a all-year crop."

Adding to the tobacco farmer's difficulties over a period of a dozen years during Stuart's early life was the tobacco war, more acutely felt in western Kentucky where the lowland crops were larger and more accessible to the *night riders*. Stuart has suggested a connection between this and the difficulty over owning hounds in his novel *Hie to the Hunters*. The freeing of "Old Dog Ring" was a campaign issue in several Kentucky elections before the hated tax on the mountaineer's dogs was repealed. The barn burner that Stuart's young heroes caught was not a night rider, however, but a crazy arsonist who loved the sight of fire.

The tobacco farmers in Greenup County, for the most part, marketed their crop in the Maysville warehouses in neighboring Mason County, hauling it by sled or wagon to the train and sending it on to Maysville. In bad weather they had to rough lock down hills so the sled would not hit the mules' heels. No part of tobacco farming was easy. Men were sometimes tempted or more or less forced to sell the crop to *pin hookers*—hardly ever to their advantage:

> . . . them Pin Hooks they rob me of my crop.
> A poor man has no chance here anymore
> Among the hills—he has to work like hell,
> And then he has a time a-tryin' to sell
> Terbacker and his lasses and his corn.
> It seems them Big Men try to rob the poor,
> For when we ask for credit from the store
> They take a lien on our terbacker crop.

And even on the regular market it was possible to lose on the crop, more heavily sometimes than the thirty-five cents a Stuart character mentions.

The farmer kept a liberal supply of the home grown *burley* and the *strong taste-bud* tobacco for his own use: many of the older hill women smoked pipes; many of the men preferred a *chaw*, saying *the taste of the Devil is better'n his broth*, meaning that the taste of the tobacco was better than the smoke. The habit of chewing gave rise to the epithet *terbacker worms* for those who were really addicted to the habit. The strong *ambeer* spittle usually hit its target *center as a die,* whether the target were a spittoon, a knot hole in the floor, a spot on the stove in a squatter shack where it would sizzle, or the eye of an enemy.

As a food crop, beans ran a close third to corn and potatoes. Yams or sweet potatoes, tomatoes, melons, sorghum molasses, and hay were sometimes taken to market, and unfortunately sometimes sold for less than it had cost to raise and prepare them for market. Few tried to raise food crops *above their usins.*

Wheat as an important food crop on the Stuarts' farm declined in the region as farmers ignorant of conservation methods wore out the land. Uncle Uglybird Skinner recalls of his own youth, the time of Stuart's grandfather, that he led the pack of *cradlers* in the wheat field:

> ". . . And young man, cradlin' is work. Ast the old men about it! We had one of the old-time threshin' machines where the hosses pulled a long sweep around and around like a cane mill and threshed the wheat."

Stuart recalls cradling wheat, shocking it, hauling it to a thresher, and later having it ground into flour. He also remembers cutting oats with a scythe on a hillside too steep and filled with stumps for a mowing machine. His grandfather, however, went back to Lawrence County on Big Sandy because he considered the Greenup County hills "no good for wheat."

The sorghum cane—which provided the family with the *long sweetenin'* of sorghum molasses, the farm animals with cane fodder (a kind of roughness), and the chickens with cane seeds—had to be harvested before frost. Like the corn fodder, the cane was easier to handle when damp with dew; and some farmers *stripped* the blades at night, using paddles to beat them down to the base of the stalks. The blades were bound into bundles and stacked so that they could later be stored in the barn. The stalks were then cut and the seed pods removed from the tops. The remaining stalks were carried to the cane mill for the molasses-making. A mule was hitched to a sweep that turned the mill, crushing the stalks into pulp, as someone sat *hunkered down* beside the mill to feed more stalks into the huge steel burrs. The green cane juice flowed into the sorghum pan, from one division to another, until it was honey-colored and ready for the barrels. Cane wood was fed at regular intervals into the furnace to keep the molasses flowing. The foam dipped with the skimmer from the pans was thrown into the *skimming hole*. Only the very last of the cane was left for the *stir-off* at the *frolickin'*.

Stuart and his father seem to have been considerably more advanced in their farming methods than most of their neighbors were. In "A Ribbon for Baldy" Stuart mentions winning a school science award for plowing a hilltop cornfield in the shape of a corkscrew—a form of contour plowing—having a single row of corn twenty-three and a half miles long. His father built up *land so poor that it wouldn't sprout black-eyed peas* by hauling leaves from the woods, filling the gullies so that the soil he was building up could not wash away; he planted cover crops and plowed them under for several successive years before he tried to raise corn, wheat, potatoes, and tobacco; and he later rotated crops. Looking at his alfalfa, his father said, "It took me thirty years to improve these old worn-out acres to make them do this!" In his last years he cleared a hilltop farm where the new ground brought especially good tomatoes, yams, and potatoes. His father seemed to have learned much from trial and error and close observation—much that is now taught through agricultural and soil-conservation programs.

Livestock—cattle, hogs, horses, sheep—and poultry were

rarely the basic source of income; but these, too, were sometimes raised for sale in an emergency or as a venture in speculation. Stuart gives rather detailed accounts of lambing, cattle raising and marketing, and hog killing.

Stuart's references to sheep include a reminiscence that his family raised their own mutton and a reference to a neighbor's shipping carloads of sheep to Cincinnati to be slaughtered. Stuart recalls *shearing days* (especially a day when a ram butted him). Women in W-Hollow spun and carded wool and wove it into cloth until the 1930s.

Anse Bushman, in *Trees of Heaven,* salted his sheep on a high cliff, where the sheep like to stay, and observed: "Daub tar on my buck's forelegs, and I'll find tar on the yowe's hips," as he realized that lambing would present difficulties in the cold, snowy weather of a mountain January. He tried to keep the ewes away from the cliffs and in the sheep barn or the windbreak during December so that he could water and feed them adequately and have the newborn lambs near the stove in the sheep shanty. In one story where the *yowes drapped their lambs* among the rock cliffs in the winter, the lambs were brought to the fireplace in the house; in *Trees of Heaven* they were warmed in heated snow water and wrapped in blankets to dry until they were ready to suckle their mothers back in the sheep pens.

In "Lean Shadows in the Valley" and in "To Market, to Market" Stuart details some of the procedures of cattle raising and marketing. The former is an account of his own unsuccessful venture in large-scale cattle raising, his failure resulting largely from bad timing in buying and selling. He uses the word *pin hookers,* usually associated with tobacco marketing, in connection with selling cattle and other stock. The method of the *pin hooker,* like that of the horse trader, has often been so clever as to deceive the farmer into a disadvantageous sale.

At the Cannongate Livestock Market the cattle were driven in front of the prospective buyers and sold to the highest bidder:

> . . . There was a floor about thirty by thirty feet square and it was covered with sawdust and shavings. On each side of the floor the seats went up like baseball bleachers, only steeper. There was a gate on the south where the cattle were let in and a gate on the north where they were let out after the bidding was over and they had been sold.

Some animals were brought in singly and some by groups; some sold by the head and some by the hundredweight. Cattle buyers lined the arena, punched the animals with their crooks, and tapped them with the leash on their quirts to keep them moving. The auctioneer "shot his words and fragments of words like bullets" into a loud-speaker until the bidding reached its peak.

The rocky slopes and long periods of cold weather and heavy indoor feeding made cattle raising in the Stuart country very difficult, so that few people raised more than they needed for their own families. Stuart's father's purchase of a registered bull was probably a good investment for himself and for the community; but the terrain still discouraged large-scale attempts at raising livestock.

Because hogs are the *hoggishest* things, as a Stuart character observed, they will eat a wider variety of foods (including *slop*), and can be cared for more easily than most other types of livestock. Few farmers in Stuart's section, however, ever raised more than enough to supply their own needs; and now some do not even find that profitable. It was unusual for a farmer to butcher twenty hogs in a season, as the Bushmans did in *Trees of Heaven*.

Hog killing of twenty fat hogs required outside help. Wood and water were hauled by sled to the spot where the hogs would be scalded, cleaned, hung up to drain, then cut up. Each hog was shot between the eyes and then stuck in the throat so that the blood could drain from an artery. With the help of a block and tackle, each was dipped into barrels of scalding water until the hair would slip, and placed on a platform of planks. The women then scraped the hair off until all were clean. The men cut the flesh around the leaders in the hogs' hind legs, and put the sharpened ends of the *gambling stick* (gambrel) behind each leader. The stick spread their legs apart and as the block and tackle lifted them into the air, their legs pulled inward on the stick, holding them securely until they could be tied to the scaffold. This scaffold was a strong hickory pole placed with one end in the forks of twin hickories and the other supported by two strong forked saplings. The *gambling stick* rested on top of the scaffold with the weight of the hog swinging below. The hogs were then gutted, drained, and pulled from the scaffold to be cut apart, and have the fat trimmed away.

The women placed the trimmings of fat in kettles over the fire to render out the lard. The men carried the hams, shoulders, and middlings to the smokehouse where they covered them with layers of salt and put them in stacks. The stacks of fresh backbones, ribs, heads, livers, spleens, hoofs, and hearts were left on the platform until the helpers had chosen what they wanted. Anse Bushman paid his helpers one dollar each for the day's work and gave them all the fresh meat they could carry home.

The landowner sometimes had difficulty in making enough to pay his taxes and buy the essential articles that he had not been able to raise for his own use; but the share cropper often had an even harder time. He had to pay one-third to one-half of the crop in grain rent and sometimes was charged a cash rent (twelve dollars looked large to a man whose cash income was almost negligible):

I rent this farm—I give one-half each year.
My landlord calls it "renting on the shear."

If I could get enough ahead I'd buy
A piece of land and then a span of mules.

I barely keep my children clothes and shoes and bread.

The landlord and the renter, or share cropper, signed a contract which they pronounced *ar-tickle,* including such details as allowing one of the children to work for cash during certain seasons, forbidding moonshining and the like, as well as declaring the amount of the cash or grain rent. The *ar-tickle* in *Trees of Heaven* even specified the number of times a week the tenant was allowed to attend revival meetings and forbade him to let his wife become pregnant!

It was especially hard for the squatters to *come under the yoke* to the extent of fulfilling such contracts. They had let their cows run out, feeding on wild pea vine during summer and dead grass in winter; their hogs ran loose and fattened on *mast;* they gardened a little; picked, canned, and sold berries; gathered nuts; dug medicinal roots and gathered *yarbs.* They hunted and fished—and made moonshine. They cut timber while the logging camps and sawmills were operating in the Hollow; but some of them refused work if they could eke out a bare subsistence without working. In their way, they had been fun loving and carefree with a precarious kind of independence. They deteriorated rapidly as they became *entangled in the spiderweb of civilization.* Illiterate and inbred, they were the type to have *simelon* (cymlin) *heads* and to get *drunk as a biled owl* when they could have been working at jobs.

The background of the squatters in the W-Hollow of Stuart's boyhood was involved with the history of timber cutting and the days of the old iron furnaces and charcoal pits in the area. Uncle Uglybird Skinner, Uncle Op Akers, the "grandpas" of Stuart's stories and autobiographies mention repeatedly those early days when the virgin timber was being cut for cordwood to make charcoal for the iron furnaces. Workers came from other parts of the country, and local timber cutters went to work in the Michigan woods or across Sandy to work in West Virginia. Each carried his ax and his little turkey of clothes across his shoulder. Boliver Tussie in *Trees of Heaven* sketches this historical background from a squatter's point of view:

> ". . . My people come here from God knows where durin' the days when they had the iron furnaces in this country. They hepped cut all the timber off'n that land. They cut big trees down fer cordwood. Jest stripped these hills bare of a sprout. The company helt the land—God knows how many companies helt it—passed it on from father to son and the big timber growed back. Now they've cut the timber agin and sawed it at the mill this time and that wasn't enough. They've sold the land to 'clear off debts,' they said. It leaves me without a home —and all our dead has been planted on that land fer the past hundred years."

Grandpa Tussie in *Taps for Private Tussie* entertains his family at the shack (after their fall from high living on Kim's insurance money) with tales of his experiences in the Michigan woods as a timber cutter.

The account of the first Mitchell Stuart partakes of tall-tale quality but at the same time has the ring of conviction. He cut timber to clear land in Lawrence County on the Big Sandy, started logging out the timber with eight yoke of oxen as soon as the snow fell, rolled the logs into Big Sandy when the river got high enough to float them down into the Ohio and on to Cincinnati and Louisville. Following a big spree, he returned home by boat to begin the cycle again.

Logging was not for weaklings or cowards. In "A Land Beyond the River" Pop and Big Jim Hailey (who paid the supreme penalty for *cuckolding* Pop) illustrate the savage code of the *water dogs* who took trains of log rafts down Big Sandy. Pop got the job of captain for a crew of water dogs "because he could holler the loudest and shoot the straightest."

> . . . I can see Pop standing there waving his hand from the front raft showing the boys the way to dodge the shoals and follow the current—great trains of logs—pine, poplars, oaks, beech, ash, maple, chestnut—great mountains of timber in them days and God knows it was the roughest place in Kentucky.

Every man in the crew had to have a gun, a pole with a spike in the end, and an agile body so that he could jump from log to log like a squirrel.

Taps for Private Tussie, with its background of World War II in the 1940s, refers to oxen *snaking logs* from the *timber woods* to the sawmill, and *lumber wagons* hauling the sawed lumber to town. The boy narrator of the novel sat on a sawed block by the *firebox* of the *steam boiler* at the sawmill and had the sawmill operator help him with his arithmetic. In "Grandpa" Mom remembers that Pap took the hardest job at the sawmill—he *offbore the slabs.* Mention is made in "Fitified Man" of the sawmill boilers going dry. These are presented as incidental details rather than a report of how a sawmill operates, possibly holding less interest for the author than those jobs that he himself had held.

Timber cutting, logging, and sawmill jobs were less foreign to the experience of the hill men than most of the other jobs open to them *on public works.* Stuart's stories span three generations of his ancestors and neighbors who worked in two different growths of timber on the hills of his region, much of which Stuart himself has now reforested in young timber.

The experienced timber cutter instructed the novice to *notch* (undercut) the tree near the ground, on the opposite side from where he would begin sawing, so that he could control to some extent the direction in which the tree fell; to square himself when he swung the ax so that an awkward stroke would turn the blade away from him, not to sink the ax so deeply in the tree that the handle would break when he tried to pull away the ax for another stroke. He taught the beginner to let his arms go limber when he swung the ax or pulled his side of the two-man crosscut saw, letting the tools do the work. Pushing the saw too hard *fornenst* the tree dulled the blade and made the work harder. When the tree began to bind the saw, the timber cutter took a *maul* and drove in a *wedge* to make the tree lean in the direction that it would fall, and make the sawing easier. One handle of the saw could be removed and the blade slipped through the tree behind the wedge. When the tree began to pop and snap, the men withdrew the crosscut quickly. *Coal oil* (kerosene) or meat rinds were used to clean resin off the saw when the timber was pine. No matter how rhythmic his movements or how expert his technique, the timber cutter built strong muscles and perspired so that he often shed his coat in freezing weather.

When cutting dead trees, such as the blighted chestnuts, the men had to be especially careful, as it was almost impossible to control the direction in which the trees fell—the brittle wood split and crashed before the men expected it. If a tree were near a cliff edge, or for any other reason had to be cut off considerably above the ground, it was also difficult to control the direction in which it fell.

A good timber cutter made from six dollars to ten dollars an acre, sometimes in addition to his *keeps* (board and room), when he cleared light timber for a local landowner, according to Stuart's story of Elliott County, "Six Sugar Maples on the Hill."

Hill boys and many hill girls learned when they were young how to swing an ax and work a crosscut. Stuart remembers getting a job in the timber woods when he was twelve years old, making railroad crossties. He received eight cents for making a number-three tie, ten cents for a number-two, and twelve cents for a number-one. Two men working together averaged about thirty ties per day for a six-day week. Stuart worked in the barn lot at home, making crossties to buy his clothes during his sophomore year in high school:

> . . . I would cut down a black oak tree. Then I would measure eight and a half feet. I would hack that place with an ax, trim the branches from the tree and measure another length and so on. Then I would measure the thickness of the crosstie on the body of the tree—hack down the sides with a broad ax. My brother would help me saw the ties apart. I would bark them and they would be ready for market.

From pioneer days *slaying the trees* was an integral part of every hill farmer's work, whether he cut timber independently for his own use or for the market, or whether he joined the *shanty-boys* or *logging crews* and worked for one of the big companies—going from one part of the country to another. In addition to all the uses of trees and saplings previously mentioned, the timber served vital functions in road construction and coal mining.

In every farmer's tool shed (smokehouse, woodshed, barn) were the timber cutter's equipment—the double-bitted ax, broad ax, crosscut saw, maul, wedge, and sledge —and in his barn was the mule or ox team to *snake out* the heavy *saw logs* or pull the *sledges* and wagons loaded with cut wood. He would probably have a *frow* (fro) for *riving* shingles and *splits* for baskets and chair seats.

The uphill work of making a profit, or even a living, on the hill farms makes it easy to understand why the men were willing to accept hazardous jobs for which they were untrained to insure themselves a cash income. This was especially true of their entering the coal mines which pocketed the mountain wall with *dark, ugly gaping mouths* and left the hills *ulcerated* with slate dumps.

Among the stories that deal primarily or incidentally with coal mining are "Vacation in Hell," which has its setting in a small privately owned coal bank having four entries; "The Anglo-Saxons of Auxierville," in which a hill mining camp is pictured; "Shadows at Dusk," which describes worn-out, broken-down hill men; "Fern," which deals with the death of a miner's daughter resulting from the same disease that had left her an orphan—tuberculosis (what is sometimes called in the coal regions *miners' asthma* is similar); "Grandpa Birdwell's Last Battle," which relates in retrospect a fight inside the coal mine.

After the crops had been laid by, the men had an interval during which they could earn enough money working in a coal mine to pay their taxes and buy winter clothes for the family. In "Vacation in Hell" the miner remarks:

> ". . . I get five cents a bushel fer diggin' th' coal and wheelin' it out where th' jolt-wagons can get to it. I can dig about thirty bushels o' coal a day on an average. That makes a dollar and a half a day. . . . It's better'n cuttin' timber fer fifty cents a thousand, or hoein' corn for seventy-five cents a day or doin' gin work fer some farmer fer fifty cents a day."

This tragic story of injury and death was written during the great economic depression of the 1930s, and has for its setting a small privately owned coal bank. The brittle rock roof had to be *posted* by the men who worked there: they cut strong white-oak trees to make *bank timbers* and did this *bank postin'* (*mine postin'*) on their own time. The men wore heavy shoes, *bank clothes* (heavy blue work shirts, jackets and pants of strong denim or some other coarse cloth), and *bank caps* with *carbite* (carbide) lamps on the front to give them light to work by a mile or more back inside the mine. They carried along their *coal forks, coal picks, shovels,* and *crowbars,* hauled them in the *jump-the-track buggy* that would be used on the return trip to bring out a load of coal. The passage was sometimes narrow, the walls and ceiling often insecure. The miners used the pick and the crowbar to loosen the vein of coal, then shoveled the coal into the buggy. Many miners fed the rats, knowing that rats will warn the miners of gas or the threat of a cave-in. In "Vacation in Hell" the men saw the rats running, realized the danger, but thought they could delay safety measures until the next day. Writing of the real-life incident on which he based the story (his father had worked in that mine where "he had to crawl on his belly like a snake"), Stuart described the horror of the slate fall succinctly: "When the farmers dug them out of the mine, they had to wade in a puddle of blood *shoe-mouth deep* to get to Ennis." The men knew the danger, knew the importance of safety precautions, but went into the mine and took chances rather than *bring their average down,* so great was their need for money.

The coal companies that brought the railroads into Big Sandy Valley operated on a much larger scale than the little home-owned drift and strip mines with only hand-powered (sometimes mule-drawn) buggies to bring the coal from the mine. Auxierville, "a pocket of earth walled in by the mountains" in the heart of the soft-coal belt, was fairly typical of such towns in the area during the second and third decades of the twentieth century. Some companies and some mines were far ahead of others in safety measures and attention to the miners' living conditions in the pre-union era of coal mining. The work and the towns, however, were obviously temporary even where the veins of coal were rich enough to be mined over a period of several generations. It is understandable that housing and working conditions were far from ideal and that the over-all effect on the hill farmers (coming from the fresh-air hardships of *corn and terbacker patchin'*) was often detrimental to both health and morale.

> . . . The mad whistles of the screeching engines on the eleven railroad tracks across the narrow-gauged valley, the zooming of the coal trucks heading for a dozen or more coal-loading ramps along the railroad spur . . .

in the shadow of the *tipple* made a noisy, dusty scene in the valley. A burning slag heap and a slate dump further marred the former beauty of the mountainside. The loaded *coal buggies* strained the heavy cables as they rolled down to the tipple.

Nearby the rows of *shotgun houses* of three and four rooms strung behind one another like the barrel of a shotgun and the squat, boxlike structures of the railroad shacks offered little of natural or man-made beauty to the large families of the miners and railroad workers who lived in them. Some ambitious men had cleared little garden patches on the steep mountainside near the tipple; and a few had a pig or a few chickens to augment their meat supply.

The people in the vicinity of Auxierville, rich in oil and natural gas as well as coal, had virtually given up farming; and most of the men who had stayed there worked for the coal companies or for the railroad.

> The boys grew into men who would . . . throttle the big engines, oil their pistons, build new tracks, and run the electric motors in the mines . . . gravel the coal with picks, coal cutters, and load it with shovels and loaders . . . in buggies and shoot the black diamonds down to the empty cars from the tipples.

They would live precariously, as Billie Auxier's account of his family illustrated:

". . . Tom, my oldest brother, wuz 'lectrocuted up thar in that coal mine. Teched a live wire with his head and that wuz the end fer 'im. . . . The company paid his funeral expenses. Then brother John . . . was kilt one night when he was a-switchin' cars over thar and a big engine backed into 'im and cut off his legs. . . . Company buried 'im purty. . . . But brother Jim, he was the fourth one down in our fambly . . . he died a-fightin'."

While the miner's daughter Fern *laid a corpse* the miners who had known her father and mother came to the *settin' up*: ". . . You can tell a coal miner at a glance, blue-mud around his knuckles and fingernails, shoulders stooped, and his face a blue-pale . . ." in the light of the kerosene lamps. These miners (among other former hill farmers who had gone into full-time jobs in industry), as Stuart illustrated in "The Anglo-Saxons of Auxierville," had their traditional culture completely upset when the boom came. Polish, Slavic, Italian, Spanish, and other European immigrants came in considerable numbers to the West Virginia coal camps; but in Stuart's region the miners were overwhelmingly of Anglo-Saxon descent and for the most part natives of Kentucky or southern West Virginia. Stuart shows awareness of the rich coal fields across Big Sandy in Mingo, Logan, and neighboring counties of West Virginia in both fiction and poetry. In poem number 83, "Mary Tongs," in *Man with a Bull-Tongue Plow*, he expresses the pathetic situation of a family when the husband and father must work away from home:

. . . My man works at the mines.
He stays away from home months at the time.
Sometimes he stays a year—It's lonesome here
For me to stay alone and milk the cows
And tend the same truck patches every year.
I wish we had money so John could stay
And be with me—John is so far away!
He's working under a West Virginia hill.

In "Shadows at Dusk," Stuart describes the men who have lost arms, legs, or otherwise been *broken down* by working in timber or in the coal mines. Coal mining continues to be an important industry along the Big Sandy on both sides of the river; working conditions have been much improved since the time of which Stuart wrote in these stories, but the fact that the great wealth of these hills served more often to impoverish and weaken than to enrich and strengthen the local population is a matter of historical record.

Closely related to coal mining (really a corollary) was railroad building. In the untitled poem number 643 of *Man with a Bull-Tongue Plow,* Stuart tells of the building of the railroad in his section of Kentucky:

> . . . And in Paul Wingbright's day
> He helped to push the forest on and pave the way;
> He helped to blast the cliffs and make the roads;
> He drove the oxen with their heavy loads;
> He helped to make crossties for these railroads,
> And drive the spikes that hold down rails of steel.

Countless references are made to the Old Line Special and the E-K Railroad. However isolated Stuart's community may have been, the people were aware of the railroad as a means of getting their tobacco to market in Maysville, and as a means of making emergency trips for family funerals and the like. Stuart presents both the ugly side of railroading and its more pleasant aspects—the former in such stories as "Accidental Death" and "Uncle Jeff"; the latter, in *Tim* and the stories of Huey the engineer, and in references to his father's work for the Chesapeake and Ohio for twenty-three years on Section 201 at Riverton, Kentucky, four miles from his home in W-Hollow.

The autobiographical story "Dark Winter" gives Stuart's family angle on a many-times-repeated situation among the hill farmers: ". . . our crops failed last year in the crawdad bottoms. . . . That is why Pop got a job on the railroad section and walks four miles to and from his work. . . ." In *The Year of My Rebirth* Stuart recalls supper-table conversations about his father's new job on the railroad:

> . . . He told us about the crew he worked with. He told us about low joints in the track, sod line, laying steel T-rails, driving spikes, tamping ties, walking track, the section foreman, the track supervisors, the superintendents, and all about his new world of railroaders and railroading.

For this work his father received World War I period wages of less than four dollars per day, which at that time seemed a fortune to him. It was a better job than digging coal or share cropping. He made $75 a month plus time and a half for sweeping snow off the switches on an overtime basis and double time (double pay) for going out on Sunday to clear away a train wreck.

The other side of the picture shows that uneducated hillmen were forced to take the jobs involving hard manual labor on the railroad:

> ". . . I told Brother Jeff to quit that damn railroad when they offered him the little pension that time. That would've been better'n stickin' it out for a few dollars on the month and endin' up in a hospital among strangers. . . ."

Pa refers to Uncle Jeff as a *broke-down man* who could have been a *boss* if he had had the education; but without it had to do hard labor on the railroad section for thirty-three years. Uncle Jeff was fatally injured when the motorcar in which he traveled as he worked on the section was hit in the fog by a Big Sandy freight train, and the other eighteen men were killed outright.

The other story (suggesting race prejudice against the *Shine* whose death was taken with grotesque lightness) also shows the hard lot of the men who worked on the section. The setting was the deep depression year of 1930 when hobos of all complexions were riding the freight trains; they rode atop the heaped-up coal on the railway cars as the trains came down Big Sandy to the Ohio River Valley:

> The sky is filled with July hotness. No one gives a damn whether he works weather like this or not. The section men don't like the smell of the cross-ties they are diggin' under the rails. They stand amid ragweeds wilted to the cinder bed—sweat streaming from their sun-cooked faces. They stand with picks in hand, and scythes in hand. They like to see the train pass so they can rest their backs. . . . They stand and thank God they have a job at $2.70 a day in this Depression.

One of them amused himself by taking a *five-spot* bet that he couldn't hit a *Shine* on one of the cars. The Negro toppled off the car, his head caved in—"accidental death," according to Corner Stone who held the inquest. The coroner was quite casual about the death, more concerned perhaps about the July heat: ". . . How can you stand hit out here nigh this rusty steel that draws like a open fireplace all the blasted hot-as-hell sun out'n Heaven?" After the required three-day period during which the dead man remained unidentified, the body unclaimed, the men gave him a pauper's burial and *got their day in* on the section.

In striking contrast to the foregoing are Stuart's hero stories, *Tim* (1939), *Huey the Engineer* (1960), and *A Ride with Huey the Engineer* (1966). A nostalgic tone pervades these stories in which hill boys along the old E-K railroad saw the engineer with an aura of glory, much as the boys in Mark Twain's *Life on the Mississippi* idealized the steamboat pilots of an earlier day. Tim was on the main line, but Huey ran the Old Line Special. Huey's long career beginning in the days of Ulysses Grant, rising to a peak of service to the country people, then declining as the automobile and truck gradually provided more convenient transportation, ended in 1930 when on the day of his death he made his final run—just before the track was taken up. Although these stories at times present naturalistic details, they are not so much pictures of the hill man at work as they are romantic legends reflecting boyish dreams.

Work in the steel mills also appeared in both prose and poetry. Poem number 618 entitled "Hog Mullins" in *Man with a Bull-Tongue Plow* suggested the ruthlessness of progress:

> By-hell I lived—I put the tree line back;
> I helped build furnaces and make the steel
> For tee-rails, spikes, and slabs of railroad cars.
> I helped to build this nation—I did wield
> The saw, the ax, the sledge, the pick and spade.

The saw, the ax, the sledge, the pick and spade. In "Rance Bushman," *Album of Destiny,* the cry of the hill man was for escape from the steel mill:

> I left the white-hot slabs of steel forever;
> I left the hooks that grab the white-hot steel . . .
> I have come home a mountain-flowing river
> To flow and flow among these pine-clad hills.
> I have returned a brother to the bluff,
> I have returned to cradle wheat and flail;
> The hell of steel has sweated me enough,
> My eyes are circled and my face is pale.
> The sun will tan my face and give me life.

In *Beyond Dark Hills* Stuart related his own experience at Armco Rolling Mills, where he began work on the *gin gang* or *bull gang* that did the odd jobs, such as cleaning out manholes, laying sewers for *privies,* unloading from the train coke and coal, picking up scraps of steel to be re-worked. Next he went in the *shed* where he was put *on the shears,* a long machine that trimmed the edges off the thick slabs of steel, next on the *oilers* (a man and two helpers flipped heavy sheets of metal), next to loading steel into boxcars, and then to a job standing beside the track down in the heat of the mills and using a long steel hook to keep the white-hot slabs of steel from running off the track. When a hook got loose on one of the cranes the white-hot steel was almost sure to kill or injure someone below. For a time he worked in the Third Division shops and then in the Second Division shops where a foundry, a machine shop, and a blacksmith shop were under one huge metal shed. He worked at the furnace where the heavy pieces of steel were heated for the air hammer:

> . . . The twenty-pound sledge hammer got my wind. . . . But I kept that job. . . . The hardest job was get-ting the hot steel out of the furnace. I always dreaded to pull down the weights and open the furnace doors. The flames threw out an intense heat. They singed my eye-brows and my eyelashes . . . one had to stand within six feet of a piece of steel six by ten inches, white hot through and through and use different kinds of cleavers.

Although Stuart realized that seven dollars a day was a good income, and that with a college education he could make much more at the mills than he could teaching school, he felt that the work had a crippling effect on mind and spirit in addition to weakening the body. After his year at the mills, working up from stand-by labor to blacksmith, he disputed with Carl Sandburg the beauty of steel.

Stuart has said more in his writings about the absence of roads into the hollow, the difficulties of travel, and the broken promises and delays about building them than he has about the hill men's helping to construct them. Among the short stories that have dealt with road building or are involved with it are "The Freeing of Jason Whiteapple," "Road Number One," and "No Petty Thief." Stuart has also published a number of articles dealing with the difficulty of building roads or getting the county or state to build roads into the Kentucky back country.

Jason, hardly literate hill man, had a passion for road building and took pride in the fact that professional engineers consulted him at times about where the roads should go in his county: "I can tell 'im if a road will stand 'r if it'll wash away," Jason simply stated a fact. He hoped to have on his tombstone: "Jason Whiteapple was a road builder. He built the roads in this county in his day. He took them from the creeks and the mudholes and put them on a higher level." Alvin Pennington is mentioned as driving a dump truck for the state highway garage after his crop was *laid by*. "He's *on the gravy train*," said Grandpa Tussie.

Judge Toodle Powell, elected on a platform of "a road for every hollow," was less dedicated to road building. *Cats* (caterpillar tractors), graders, and trucks were more misused than used by incompetent men hired for the construction work because of their political affiliations rather than for their ability. Stuart himself had the first road built into his hollow.

In "No Petty Thief" the man who stole a power shovel from the road-building crew commented on the scarcity of good roads into the hills:

> . . . It was a real road they were making. They were going down into the deep valleys and around the rocky walled mountains and over the mountains. . . . And if the contractors could've only finished the big road and covered it with loose gravel before November, we'd a-had a real road that people could've driven automobiles over. . . . I've never seen one of 'em.

He explained that temptation came his way when the road-building crew had to stop work during the November rains. Before the mud made it impossible to move the equipment, they took the dump trucks, caterpillar tractors, and the big graders back to town; but possibly because they feared that big power shovel would bog down they left it "a-settin' there lonesome-like." This stalling of the work often made rural roads impassable for months.

The Stuarts, after building their own road, saw the big trucks break down their little bridges and make their road considerably worse before the county made a better road—after World War II. Although the roads in the hill counties of northeastern Kentucky are still far from perfect, it is unlikely that anyone with an automobile would not be able to get to town at any time of the year that his town neighbors could drive safely.

Other jobs were available from time to time for strong and energetic hill boys and men. During his boyhood Stuart—in response to a call for farm boys to help overhaul the town of Greenup—did construction work for thirty cents an hour for a ten-hour day. Three husky farm boys *white-eyed* on the job, but Stuart stopped only because he had decided to enter high school.

Stuart's basic portrait of the hill man during his own youth showed him to be hard-working, self-respecting, and self-sustaining; only toward the end of the era did some of the less energetic hill men deteriorate under the influence of government work and relief programs—a phase of hill life that Stuart has treated humorously, but with many tragic overtones, in *Taps for Private Tussie.*

Stuart has been able to write vividly and specifically of many types of work and virtually all phases of farm work on the basis of firsthand experience. He sees in most of these the paradox of bane and blessing, of a means of livelihood inextricably involved with a loss of solitude and beauty. From time to time in poems and stories he refers to hill boys and girls who have left for better living and working opportunities elsewhere; and he has heartily encouraged the young hill people to get an education and develop their full potentialities as individuals and as citizens; but it is a rare story, essay, or poem that does not imply or state the nourishing, healing, restoring power of nature for those who return *to drink of lonesome waters.*

In "Ben Tuttle," the closing poem in the collection *Kentucky Is my Land,* Stuart is paying tribute to a man who retimbered denuded ditch-scarred ugly slopes and brought beauty to his hills and deep contentment to himself as he contributed "mastpoles for a thousand ships," "telephone and electric poles for a thousand miles of wire," and "fence posts to reach across this State." A man who sold only trees that had their growth and reset a young tree for every one he had cut was fulfilling Stuart's concept of what all phases of the hill man's work should be—constructive utilization of resources and conservation of what is best not only in the natural resources of the hills themselves, but also what is best in the character of the men who do the work. When work affects men or nature otherwise, Stuart cannot see in it true progress.

CHAPTER SIX

Folk Life in a Primitive Setting

. . . the road that leads to W-Hollow is a wagon road, the first three miles of it. For the rest it's a cowpath, a rabbit path, a mule path . . . a place under the sun walled in by the wind and the hills.

HEAD O' W-HOLLOW

Whether Jesse Stuart takes his readers on a tour of country farms, mountain revival meetings, schools, frolics, or workings, the mountain setting is everywhere apparent. The poetic beauty of Nature through the cycle of the seasons has tempered the artist and his art. Even when he focuses on incongruities and grotesque details for his comedy or tragedy, his strongly folk-flavored language draws its strength from the soil. His metaphor inevitably turns to trees, flowers, crops, hills, forest, birds, and animals. And when he peoples the scene, it is with people of the soil, people who think and speak in terms of seed time or harvest time. Their fathers and fathers' fathers before them thought and spoke so, for their now nearly vanished folkways lingered overlong in Jesse Stuart's Kentucky, so long that they became a liability instead of the asset they had been in the pioneer beginnings.

Stuart drew liberally from the recollections of his elders as well as from his own observations, and from these he has projected the chronicles of W-Hollow from early settlement to the present. His writing presents a regional folk museum containing variety and detail unsurpassed in American literature.

A composite picture of a hill farm emerges from descriptions of the eight farms on which the Stuarts lived and the homes of their neighbors. The typical farm had little in common with the squalor of the dirt-floored, *rubber-roy* roofed slab shanties in which the timber cutters lived; nor did it have much in common with Uncle Amos Batson's twelve-room two-story white frame house in Lonesome Valley.

The typical log shack, which was really better than the word *shack* implies, was built in the manner described in the short story "Wilburn":

> . . . Mom and the neighbor women fixed a big dinner for the men out under the pine tree. . . . The men lifted the big logs and skidded them up poles onto the square pen of pine, poplar, oak, and chestnut logs. They lifted a big house log upon the skids. Two men pulled the log with a rope from one corner of the house and then from the other corner. . . . When the corner of the long house log was pulled upon the frame of logs . . . Wilburn took his ax and started notching the log. The chips flew.

Very likely they also hand rived the roof shingles with a *frow*. No detailed description is given of the completed house, but since it had a center chimney, it surely had two large rooms in the big house besides the kitchen and the loft. As a family grew, other rooms were added.

The typical house had a lean-to kitchen, separated from the main part of the house by a *dogtrot*, which aided ventilation; in some two-story log houses, an *upper dogtrot* served the same purpose. If the loft, or upstairs, had been floored, it was used as a sleeping room or for storage; access was by a crude stairway or sometimes merely a ladder to the *scuttle hole*. Either at the front or back of the house (or both) was a porch. Even in Stuart's time windows, which had to be bought in town, were rare, though few homes had only one window. The floors were *puncheon*, with home-made woven or hooked rag rugs scattered here and there. The walls were covered in some way, if only with news-papers or pictures cut from seed catalogues and other ad-vertising matter circulated in the hills. In many homes the big family pictures in rococo frames showed that the itiner-ant photographers had at some time passed through the re-gion. Most people had in this main room a Bible and a gun. Lighting was from kerosene oil lamps. Sometimes a pine torch lighted the way across the *dogtrot*.

A rock chimney and a big rock fireplace with a mantel-piece over it was the family gathering place in winter; and the *jamm-rock* of the fireplace was a good place to strike matches or knock the ashes from a pipe. The women knitted, pieced quilts, or sewed; the men whittled, smoked, or talked of the crops, livestock, and experiences of the day. In some families singing, fiddling, or tale telling whiled away the winter evenings. The poker, *coal scoop* (or coal bucket), and the *fire shovel* were close by. Sometimes the churn stood on the hearth so that the heat would *clabber* the milk faster. One of the children often knelt in front of the fire and popped a *capper* of corn, or roasted sweet pota-toes or some other food in the ashes. In some stories the terms *fore-stick* and *back-stick* are used instead of *fore-log* and *back-log*. It was the only source of heat for the main part of the house.

The most notable articles of *house plunder* (the word furniture is used with about equal frequency in Stuart) in Stuart's community as throughout the highlands were beds. *Cord beds* or *slat beds* with homemade *bed ticks* filled with feathers, straw, corn shucks, broom sage, or even oak leaves for mattresses might number three or four in a room.

Benches, stools, and *hickory split-bottom chairs* (usually including a rocking chair near the fireplace) were strong and durable, if not of much aesthetic value. A *stand table* and perhaps a *dresser* completed the basic furnishings of the *front room*. In some houses the women used *kivers* on these and on the *mantelpiece*. Nails and shelves along the wall were hill substitutes for wardrobe and closet space. If company came, the children were given *pallets* of folded quilts to sleep on the floor. If boys slept in the hayloft on cold winter nights with hound dogs for warmth, it was probably boyish adventure rather than necessity that prompted them.

If the family did not have a *smokehouse* (the average family did), *leatherbritches beans,* strings of red peppers, and drying herbs were tied to the rafters in the main room or to nails in the kitchen. Although the furniture was sparse, the house was fully occupied—with families of six to a dozen occupying three or four rooms (including kitchen and loft).

By Stuart's time the heavy iron kitchen stove, or range, had replaced the fireplace for most of the cooking. On it was a teakettle full of hot water, and the *biler of coffee* was usually filled several times during the day. The teakettle and a galvanized water bucket on a bench or table nearby provided the family supply of hot and cold water. The *wash pan,* facetiously called by some Stuart characters *the dabblin' pan,* was usually kept near the water bucket—on the back porch in summer, in the kitchen in winter. For baths the galvanized washtub came into use. Dirty water, except dish water which was added to the hog *slop,* was thrown over the hill or into the weeds. Second to the stove was the sturdy table (usually covered with oilcloth) in the kitchen; some could be expanded to accommodate a large number of people on special occasions and for *workin's.* Benches or chairs, perhaps a flour barrel if the family raised wheat, gourds containing soda, salt, etc., hanging near the stove, and the woodbox; and some sort of cupboard or *safe* completed the kitchen furnishings. A mirror of sorts usually hung in the kitchen or on the porch for the men to shave by and comb their hair.

The front yard nearly always had shade trees, grass, and flowers—old-fashioned roses, hollyhocks, blue flags, and others to supply *flowerpots* for the house in summer—and was enclosed by a paling fence, the gate held shut by weights (some used worn-out plow points for the purpose). At the back of the house was the cleanly swept *chip yard* with its pile of logs to be split into firewood, and the ax in the chopping block beside the woodpile. The laundry equipment was there: the tub or barrel that caught rainwater from the drain pipe at the corner of the house; the big black iron wash kettle; the *ash hopper* that was essential in making strong homemade soap; a stool for the galvanized washtub to sit on while the hill woman rubbed the clothes to whiteness on a brass washboard (it made her hands rough as a *gritter*); the clotheslines tied from one tree to another, and supported by a forked pole, or *sprout*. Many hill families kept the grindstone in the chip yard to be convenient for sharpening household knives as well as farm tools. Benches served the family as a place to sit and string beans, peel apples, whittle, or just talk; it was at times a sort of outdoor family room, with the children playing as the older people worked or talked. Along the garden fence vined gourds that would later dry out and be used for salt and soda containers and for dippers. Most families encouraged songbirds to build nests near the house by improvising birdhouses for them on garden fence posts—bluebirds, wrens, martins, and others. Hunters sometimes housed their hound dogs in a lean-to beside the barn and sometimes in the back yard. It was at times the scene of serious family conversations.

Near most houses was a well or spring, the well box often consisting of a section of log called a *well gum,* with a wooden or galvanized bucket hanging on the *well sweep* and a *gourd dipper* hanging on a nearby sprout for the use of any passerby whose *biler might be dry.* The well had almost surely been located by a *water witch* with a peach-tree fork. Nearby also was the stone earth-floored *cellar* where canned fruit, home-rendered lard, milk and butter, eggs, and other foods needing cool dampness were stored. Above the cellar, or in a separate structure nearby, was the *smoke-house* where cured hams (smoked with green hickory), *middlings* (*middinmeat*), *sow-belly, jowl,* dried fruits, and vegetables, some of the laundry and gardening equipment, and the rag bag were kept. Most farmers had near the house a row of beehives, or *bee-gums.* At some distance from the house was the *privy,* for indoor toilets were virtually unknown in rural sections of the hills even a generation ago. Only the most shiftless hill people lacked outdoor toilets.

A little farther from the house were the *milk gap,* the hogpen, and the barn where the cattle, mules, or horses, feed for the livestock, and most of the farm equipment were housed. Tobacco farmers sometimes had an extra barn for tobacco until it was ready for market and then used the same barn for sheep in the winter at lambing time. With a few *cow brutes,* a span of rabbit mules, a *gang of chickens,* a *brood sow,* and some *fattenin' hogs;* with corn in the crib, fodder and hay in the barn loft, and food for the family holed up, canned, dried, and ground; with enough money from his tobacco crop to pay his taxes and buy salt, pepper, coffee, and occasionally some dry goods and thread—the farmer felt reasonably secure and happy.

The fields were once fenced with oak or chestnut rails, *staked-and-ridered*—some of them standing for several generations—but by Stuart's time a three- or four-strand barbed-wire fence tightly drawn and stapled to locust posts was the usual way of enclosing fields and marking boundary lines. The old rail fences and the cruder brush fences went up in the smoke of forest fires.

Stuart saw humor in incidents relating to farm life—when a runt pig that looked like a blue-tick hound pup learned to milk cows; in Pa's making a profit by selling and buying back a bull that frightened everyone except Pa by walking around on his hind legs, as Pa had taught him to do when he was a young bull calf. He saw pathos in the behavior of a mule when her companion at the plow died. He saw dark tragedy in a mother's trying to have her baby alone while her husband was too late returning with the doctor on muleback—"The unfed hounds and the unslopped hogs had come into the shack and had eaten part of her flesh and nearly all of the baby." The grotesque incidents along with the everyday ones contribute to an authentic account of the only life possible in an isolated and primitive setting.

The basic diet of corn bread, pork, buttermilk, and sorghum molasses—even when supplemented by biscuits in the wheat-growing Stuart family and by apples and wild fruits, wild meat, dried and canned vegetables—Stuart recognized in later life to have been deficient in certain respects; but such *country grub* that would *stick to your ribs* satisfied their appetites and gave them energy for the hard work on the farm. The abundant apples tempted *younguns* to eat too many when they were too green, sometimes causing *summer complaint* or *collarmoggis*, but it is not unusual for a former hill resident to have his mouth water for apples from a certain tree that grew on his farm.

While they were living on rented farms the Stuarts had variable fortunes, sometimes so poor that *bumblebee corn* grew on the hill slope and the *crawdads* cut the roots of the plants growing in the *creek bottoms,* and their pigs were so far from fat that the family joked about not getting the washtub too close to the gambrel when they butchered for fear they would lose sight of the hog altogether. They prospered much more after Mitchell Stuart bought those first fifty acres, where they set out young orchards and berries and continually made improvements on the buildings and the land:

> We raised fat porkers for our own use and to sell. We had mutton and our own beef. My mother and sisters canned hundreds of quarts of wild blackberries, strawberries, raspberries, dewberries, and apples, and made apple butter and pumpkin butter. . . . We raised sweet and Irish potatoes. We raised corn to feed the livestock and fatten our hogs. We raised wheat on our hills. . . . We raised cane for sorghum which we often substituted for sugar.

When Stuart mentions *long sweetenin'*, it is usually in a figurative sense, as in Kim Tussie's love-making to Vittie. He more often refers to sorghum, molasses, or lassies (according to what type of character is speaking). This sugar substitute along with the honey from wild bees was for generations the customary sweetening throughout the highlands, and Stuart has neighbors who prefer it today.

One of the biggest outlays of food in all his writings—no doubt suggesting how good his mother's cooking tasted to him after he had been away for a few months—was the Christmas dinner at the Stuart home during Jesse's freshman year at Lincoln Memorial University. Whatever an outlander's opinion of the food might be, Jesse must have felt that the food and the welcome from his family justified the harrowing trip home—hitchhiking with a madman, spending a winter night sleeping in a henhouse, being threatened with dire punishment if he did not pay his train fare when he had tried to hide in the toilet. "This ain't *food*, son. This is old country *grub*," said his father:

. . . spare ribs, ham, gravy, sweet milk and buttermilk, roasted goose, chicken, blackberries, strawberries, cherries, apples, huckleberry preserves, wild grapes, jelly, honey, biscuit and corn bread, pickled beans, pickled corn, and kraut, pie, cake, and quail meat extra.

Another feast was the last supper with Big Eif before he fulfilled his death token by dying at ten o'clock that night, a meal that included ham, goose, quail, rabbit, hens, ducks, dumplings, corndodger, potatoes, fall beans, soup beans, and leatherbritches, half-a-dozen kinds of jams and jellies, fruits, pies, cakes, with wine and home-grown taste-bud tobacco to finish on. A similar show of bounty prevailed at the *basket dinner* before it gave way to a feuding fight: the *awfulest lot of cooking* included turkey, squirrel, several kinds of pickles, preserves, and similar articles to those listed above. Onions, pumpkin, radishes, turnips, possum meat, coon meat, and various other dishes are mentioned here and there in his writings. At hog-killing time the hill people considered backbones and spareribs special treats, and some liked the heart and liver. None of it was wasted. Such feasts as those mentioned were not the everyday fare, but hill women took pride in the number of dishes prepared for special events; having plenty to eat, however limited or varied the menu, was of utmost importance to people whose very existence depended to a great extent on physical energy.

Stuart gives no recipes for preserving foods, but he mentions the old *sulphurin' barrel* for *sulphuring apples;* holing up potatoes and other vegetables; drying sliced apples on the clapboard roof of a smokehouse, with a quilt frame to catch the slices if they slide off; meat curing; canning, preserving and making jellies, which belong to the end of an era.

It was possible for a hill family to raise virtually all of their food except salt, pepper, and coffee. Stuart feels nostalgia for the passing traditional ways of preserving and preparing foods, as he does for other folk traditions lost or swiftly passing; but he sees much to compensate for these losses in the convenience of having winter roads (hard-surfaced or graveled) and improved living conditions.

Stuart's account of the way his people dressed shows the same blending of tradition with adaptation to the local environment that was evident in their food habits and details of their house furnishings and surroundings. The men's clothing particularly was functional rather than decorative, although both younger and older men had their small vanities of dress for special occasions. The everyday outfit except in cold weather included coarse blue work shirt (sometimes with darker crisscross stripes where the overall suspenders have kept the sun from fading them), overalls, red or blue bandannas, brogan shoes, and one of three types of head gear—a cap with a bill, a wide-brimmed straw hat, or the slouch black umbrella hat familiar throughout the highlands in all seasons. In cool weather the men added an overall jumper, or jacket.

Stuart could not recall a time when his father did not wear such an outfit when he went to Greenup on Saturdays: ". . . overalls, clean blue work shirt, overall jacket, his soiled weathered cap with a shrinking bill, and his turned-up-at-the-toe stump-scarred brogan shoes."

Some hill men did not wear underwear during the hot weather, a practice that contributed a grotesquely amusing incident to Stuart's repertory of stories. At a Holy Roller meeting some pranksters cut the preacher's suspenders, exposing him in only his shirt and shoes and dispersing an already hysterical congregation.

In really cold weather the hill men wore long woolen or cotton fleece-lined underwear, heavy yarn socks, brogans or boots, wool shirts or sweaters, sheep lined or heavy wool coats, wool scarves, woolen caps pulled down over their ears, wool or fur-lined mittens or gloves. Corduroy came into popularity about the time Stuart was growing up, for it was cheap and reasonably warm. Not everyone could afford to dress so warmly, but winters in the hills were and are damp and cold with much sleet and snow and winds *keen as a razor blade.*

The outfit that the narrator wore to the hanging—a very special occasion for impressing boys and girls alike—was probably the outfit of a hill sport of Jesse Stuart's father's youth: high-heeled button shoes and a powder-blue, double-breasted suit with peglegs. Bollie Beaver wore such a powder-blue serge suit to the *molasses-making;* and old Anse Bushman wore a very similar one when he dressed up to go to a court session, with the added items of a high cel-luloid collar, broad striped necktie, and a watch chain and fob over his vest. For a hill dance most of the young men wore tight-fitting pants (Stuart often specified blue serge), wool coats not necessarily matching the pants, and carried pistols that showed out of their holsters when their coattails flapped up in the lusty action of the square dance. Most mountain men preferred *galluses* (suspenders) to belts. Elster wears to the *Baptis' Footwashing* somewhat more modern apparel: a clean white starched shirt, a blue neck-tie, blue serge pants, and black slippers. Stuart's account of Pa, Finn, and Shan going into Ferton (probably Hunting-ton), West Virginia, to see Uncle Jeff reflects the poverty of the average hill man's wardrobe of a generation ago:

> . . . People do look at us and Pa gets hot behind the collar. . . . He [wears] . . . a big gray overcoat . . . that strikes him around the ankles. I found the overcoat in an old house and gave it to him . . . and my old blue overcoat strikes [Finn] . . . about five inches above the knees. . . . I have a new overcoat. . . . Pa's hair is out a little long and it rolls up a little at the edge of his thick felt black cap. . . .

Allowing for humorous exaggeration, the person familiar with hill life knows that older hill men used to be reluctant enough about spending money for dress clothes to make this picture credible almost to the last detail.

The hill man's custom of sleeping *in his shirttail,* repeatedly mentioned in Stuart's stories, and the identification of death with sleeping inspired Stuart's first published story "Battle Keaton Dies," in which the aged *figure of earth* made a deathbed request (respected with superstitious awe) that he be buried in his long underwear and a clean blue work shirt. Lack of privacy led to the common practice of dressing and undressing under the covers; and perhaps the early hour of rising contributed to the custom of sleeping partly clad in daytime clothes.

Using the same focus that he has used for other aspects of hill life, Stuart describes the characteristic women's clothing of his early boyhood and his parents' earlier life. Gone were the spinning wheel and loom from most mountain homes, and with them the strong homespun clothes; in their place women wore cheap cotton dresses which they bought from the mail-order houses or made from cloth bought at the nearest general store.

Older women wore *slat bonnets* tied under their chins, flat-heeled comfortable shoes (sometimes brogans for field and garden work), and high-necked, long-sleeved dresses, with aprons tied tightly around their waists and reaching almost to the bottom of their ankle-length dresses. And in almost every story they *crumble their burley in their apron pockets.* For work in the fields and around the house the women—men, too—sometimes went barefoot in warm weather or wore shoes without stockings. Except that the clothes the women wore for dress were newer and cleaner, they looked much the same as those worn at home. They usually had one outfit, including a pair of shoes, that they *saved* to wear when they *went places.* Notice the outfit (one that had been a favorite of hers) that Brother Fain Groan brought to the Kale Nelson Graveyard when he tried to resurrect his dead wife: high-crowned hat with a goose plume on one side, peaked-toe patent-leather low-heeled button shoes, a dress with white dots. The timber cutter evokes a familiar mountain picture when he remembers holding to his mother's dress tail as she walked up the furrowed new ground to hoe terbacker with his father—she wore a white dress with black dots and a slat bonnet. In a recent story Stuart describes the women of the Old-Fashioned Faith who wear trailing black dresses with sleeves to their wrists as turning back the clock to another day and another time. He makes a rare mention of Mom's wearing a blue dress trimmed in white frilly laces to the Fourth-of-July celebration in Blakesburg: only women and girls of questionable character had fancy clothes and impressive wardrobes, according to hill belief. Symanthia's having *six right pretty dresses* after she had been sweeping out the timber cutters' shanties aroused a big question in the mind of Finn's mother.

The young girls, such as Subrinea Tussie at the molasses-making, also wore cotton dresses, usually in brighter colors and a good deal shorter than their mothers wore. Subrinea wore no stockings with her slippers. Shoes were expensive and had to be taken care of. Stuart remembers that his sister carried hers within sight of church before putting them on. The increasing interest in good clothes is a recurrent motif in Stuart's stories, perhaps because he, his brother, and sisters were conspicuous at high school because of their poor clothes. In one story a share cropper's daughter ordered, with the help of huckster Charlie, an outfit that made her look like a girl in the mail-order house catalogue, elsewhere called the *Wish Book,* and paid for it on the installment plan. She was so successful that she won back her beau whose attention had wandered to the landowner's daughter. In accordance with Grandpa Doug Grayhouse's will, all members of his family (men, women, and children) ordered outfits from the *Wish Book*, as he had marked them, using the money that he had bequeathed them for the purpose.

On cool mornings and evenings the older women wore shawls. Most of the women and girls wore heavy sweaters in winter under their old coats, and, as they did in summer, had one good outfit for the season.

"Mom made all the clothes we wore" was true in many families. The boy then described his own little pair of knee pants that buttoned onto his shirt, and his twelve-year-old sister's white dress with a sash of red ribbon tied in a big bowknot "like Mom dressed her when we went to Plum Grove's Children's Day once a year." These little home-made boys' suits were the usual dress for little boys past the shirttail stage. All children in the hills went barefoot from April until October—to save shoes and because they liked it.

"Homespun jeans and linsey have given way to shoddy 'store clothes,'" wrote Horace Kephart, and perhaps the cheap ginghams, percales, and calicoes that the hill women could afford were shoddy; but buying them instead of spinning, carding, and weaving when the isolation from the outside world pointed toward an easier way to clothe themselves was part of their adaptation. In Stuart's boyhood, this adaptation was still to their own way of life in their own setting. Until the communication lines were fully open—although the traditional way of doing things was modified—the hill people made little conscious effort to imitate in their clothing or in any other phase of their living the ways of the people down in the *level land*.

The hill people of Stuart's boyhood were different from *outlanders* not merely in having mud on their feet, in eating sorghum and corn bread, in having *dogtrots* and *scuttle holes* in their houses; they were different in the way they *looked at* and *listened to* people and to the wild life of their environment—and Stuart makes his readers aware that the closeness to nature compensated much for the loneliness. They were different, too, in their freedom from the *kind* of conventionality found in American small towns. They had their own code of morality, religion, and community life; but it allowed room for extremes of individualism within the over-all pattern.

Stuart shows the hill setting from the viewpoints that he held himself, but also from those of people whom he knew intimately—his father, his mother, his grandfather Hilton, his old squatter friend on Laurel Ridge, the old gravedigger and water witch, the wild young bucks, the young people who were ambitious to leave the hills—and many more.

The following details of the hill setting are a composite, as the foregoing section of this chapter has been, showing how different types of hill people reacted and responded to their native hills in different seasons and under different circumstances.

"The hills form a semicircle barrier against roads"—a protective barrier against the pressures of a rapidly developing American civilization but at the same time a barrier obstructing progress. Although the hills above Big and Little Sandy are not very high, they are steep, with sandstone cliffs sheering off unexpectedly from forests of *tough-butted white oaks,* waist-high briar thickets, tangled vines, and thick undergrowth at almost every turn in the narrow *snake-paths.* Deeply cut by numerous tributary streams to the rivers, snake-infested in summer, icy and snow-covered in winter, they were and are a hazard to both man and beast in any season. Tarvin Bushman was not exaggerating the hazardous nature of his trip from the house to the sheep shanty in winter:

> I've been in our cornfield and didn't know it. I come out
> the left spur back yander on the ridge instead of the right.
> If I'd gone over the hill I would a-been among the Artner
> woods and cliffs. . . . Maybe I'd a-been a mess fer the
> hungry crows, buzzards, and foxes.

A grim folk-flavored humor, as in the foregoing quotation,
appears frequently in Stuart's writings. Stuart describes the
hills as dark, desolate, rock-ribbed, sprouty, tumbled, bat-
tered, scarred, lonesome, and drab; but he speaks of them
also, as pine-clad, fern-clad, homey, fair green hills, and
grassy uplands with rhododendron hanging from the cliffs.
In winter at Plum Grove the snow makes a *great white quilt
over the monster mountains and their baby hills.* In any
season the terrain discouraged travel, but to the hill man
who had learned to love loneliness the hills had a kind of
beauty in all seasons.

Stuart describes the *rock cliffs* as variously as the hills of
which they are a part: jagged, jutted, defensive crags, *giant
rocks like scaly monsters sleeping in the sun;* but a different
connotation occurred to a native son who had been absent
for a time and returned—the hills seemed to offer *security
as great as mountain rocks.* Even when Stuart is coining his
own similes and metaphors, they often have a folk flavor:
one's *backbone must be hard as stone to bend; love must
stand as cliffs have stood against the hands of time, of
freeze and sleet; and men can be as kind or as cruel as the
hills that have made them.*

In the spring, blue mountain water fills every ravine with
rushing waters and every gorge with a roaring torrent
tumbling "over rock ledges down the steep, rugged slope to
Sandy River." The *lonesome waters* go *moaning over stones,*
murmuring, mumbling, laughing; they are slush waters,
unvexed mountain water, glossy green beneath the willows,
kissing the pebbled shore. For the hill people these streams
flowing to some mysterious outland place have had as much

fascination as the sea has for coast-line and island people. Their names are typical of the highlands: Slush Creek, Shinglemill Creek, Shacklerun, Hoods Run, Duck Puddle, Academy Branch, Cedar Riffles, Put-Off Ford, W-Hollow Creek (because it curves in the shape of the letter "W"), and Little Sandy. Stuart pays high compliments to beauty and character with the phrase *clear* (or *pure*) as *blue mountain water*, but he knows the harmful effects that can result from drinking *lonesome waters*:

> . . . blue water in the setting September sun, water beautiful to see but treacherous to drink. It had put me flat on my back twice. . . . Uncle Rank had just told me I *would come back to drink of lonesome water* before I died. Why didn't he say I would come home and drink of lonesome water and die?

This clear mountain water that looked so pure took its toll of typhoid victims, a fact the hill people, who judged water by its appearance and taste, were loath to accept.

The mountain streams were a source of food and of pleasure; they were the only bathtubs some mountain men and boys knew; they gave rise to tall tales; and, most important of all to the hill people, they were the way out of the remote hills and hollows to other neighborhoods and the outside world. The wagon road crossed the streams repeatedly in the shallow places, and the footpath led across crude foot logs made from felled trees or split logs.

"Every hill, hollow, stream, wood, road, fence, cemetery, or rock is kept definitely in mind as it actually exists" when Stuart writes of his region, remarked Lee Oly Ramey, early Stuart biographer. In *Trees of Heaven*, his earliest novel, he describes the entire cycle of seasons as they come to the Hollow. In many poems he writes of the wind whispering through the summer grass, through the trees like the music of a far-off violin, rattling the autumn leaves, cutting like a knife as it brings the sleet, snow, and ice of winter. He knows and has written of the droughts that produced *bumblebee corn* and of cloudbursts that washed out *gully-ditches deep enough to bury a mule*. As he watches an autumn dawn it seems to him that his mountain world is like a giant waking:

> Watching him rub sleep from his eyes
> With rockcliff knuckles,
> Mountain range arm
> Broad, calloused, plateau hand
> Clayfingered down into the ridgeline spurs.

The giant is not always amiable. Stuart has communicated the hill man's dependence upon the unpredictable and often freakish acts of nature. He has reflected the inseparable blending of the hill man's feeling for nature with superstition and religion. "We come for a season like the sweet William," Mom explained to a small boy why his brother had to die. But death and desolation in some seasons of the year and of Stuart's life have not blinded him to the beauty there.

Nowhere is Stuart more the poet in his appreciation of nature than when he writes of April bringing spring to W-Hollow. He has written of "those golden sprays of warm spring sunshine on white and pink crab apple blossoms, redbud, wild plum, and *white lilting sails* of dogwood that spread in the wind over the Kentucky hills in April."

> Then came the sawbriar and the greenbriar leaves
> And the trailing arbutus on the rock-ribbed hills.
> Next came the snowwhite blossoms of percoon in the
> coves.

The *percoon*, opening its transient, delicate petals in March before the threat of snow is past, has always been a favorite with Stuart. It recurs when he is speaking in his own person and in countless other poems and many stories in which a love for the flower is attributed to others. His wife prefers

the wild primrose that grows beside the lichen-gray sandstone. Repeatedly, too, Stuart writes of wild sweet Wil-
liams, daisies, roses, and others—he seems to love every
wild flower that grows in the hills. Among the many wild
flowers mentioned in his writings are the woodland rose,
mountain daisy, dandelions, wild iris, wild pansies, blue
ageratum, violets, trillium, dusty miller, thick ferns, and in
autumn the purple ironweed, "like a great purple robe
spread over the landscape," goldenrod, queen of the mea-
dow (joe-pye), and farewell-summer. The folk names are
picturesque, but sometimes make it difficult to learn the
botanical names: *babytears* (bluets), *needle-and-thread*,
lady slipper, whippoorwill flowers, Johnny-jump-up, wind
flowers, blue-blooming beggar lice, oxeye daisies, *chigger
daisies, devil's shoestrings* (with bright orange trumpet-
shaped flowers), and silkweed.

The wild flowers overlap with weeds, and most of the old-
timers believed that "every weed, tree, flower, shrub, and
plant was put here by the Creator of this universe for a purpose." Even the sassafras prevents soil erosion. In his appreciation of hill wild flowers, Stuart is an *oddling* only in that
he is more articulate than most hill people. He draws both
folk and original similes from nature, *hairlike love-vines on
a fence* becoming almost as familiar to his reader as *percoon*. To grasp the aptness of the simile, one must see the
hairlike stems closely vined upon a fence, red-gold in summer and black after the first frost.

Other weeds also have interesting folk names: *careless*, a
weed that will grow almost anywhere, the hybridus ama-
ranthus; *life-everlasting*, with its gray leaves resembling rabbits' tails, getting its name perhaps from its medicinal uses;
pig ear, mouse's ear, snakeroot (which smells to city-bred
Alf like the city dump), horseweed, stickerweed, cockleburs, shoe makes (sumac), boneset, milkweed, foxglove,
wild Indian turnip, chickweed on which the redbirds feed,

pussy willow, Jimson (Jamestown) weed, pennyrile (pennyroyal) with its pungent scent and insect-killing powers, pusley (purslane), ragweed, smartweed, wild honeysuckle, wild pea vine like a green plush carpet, May-apple, and alders.

A good deal of humor resulted in one of Stuart's stories when a drunken man was tied onto a mule that had cockleburs under the saddle; not knowing about the cockleburs, the man thought it was a judgment sent on him for his wicked ways when the mule began to buck, and promised God that he would change his ways if only he could get safely off the mule. He did, and his son unobtrusively discovered and removed the burs. Weeds produce humorous effects in several Stuart stories.

Some would also classify as weeds the *sallet greens* that vary the long winter's diet. In April even now mountain women take a *case knife* and a basket out to the rich patches along the clearings and cut a mess of greens: tender shoots of pokeweed, watercress (sometimes called creases), young plantain, wild beet, narrow dock, pepper grass, sweet anise (Sweet Annies), willie britches (white-top), sheepshower (sheep sorrel). Those who know how to distinguish what is edible from what is poisonous have more than a hundred varieties to choose from, says Stuart. Boliver Tussie expressed the general enthusiasm of the hill people for greens, "I jest love to eat greens biled with fat meat." Some added vinegar and raw onions.

Yarbs as well as *sallets* make use of many weed and flower leaves, roots, and flowers. At all seasons the old folks gathered them for teas, salves, poultices, and tonics. Medical authorities have long denied the efficacy of ginseng for heart ailments and other diseases, but *sangin'* is still a source of income in the hills. (Note that Stuart calls one of his characters, a sharp trader, Ginsang Tootle.) Modern medicine has supported some of the herb preparations of the hill

people, but to a great extent herb medicine has been rele-
gated to folklore. Stuart is aware of the poison ivy and hay-
fever-provoking ragweed, but thinks few people who live
close to the soil are affected by them.

Among the many expressions relating to plants are Stuart's use of the folk simile *grow like a weed* (which has a
special meaning to those who have *murdered weeds* day
after day in the July heat of the cornfield); of *growed up
like a hickory sprout* to describe an adolescent; *root, leaf,
and branch* to express riddance; *time is a witherin'* [*us*] *on
the stem* (certainly as image making as *vine* in the folk expression; *limber as a wilted milkweed* aptly describes a
drunken farmer's long, skinny neck; *straight as a sourwood
sprout* (a Stuart coinage so descriptive that it could easily
become a folk cliché); *like a tuft of dead bull grass* of a
man's unkempt mustache; *sharp as locust thorns* of a rooster's spurs, localizing an old chiché, *sharp as a thorn*, as does
clean as a pawpaw whistle to describe a garden that has
just been hoed, or *got out of the weeds.*

The hill man has developed a taste for wild fruits of such
native trees and shrubs as the persimmon, pawpaw (not the
papaya of tropical climates), wild plum, wild cherry, crab-
apple; for the wild strawberries, blackberries, grapes, and
huckleberries (among which rattlesnakes have their dens);
for hickory nuts, butternuts, hazelnuts, and black walnuts;
as well as for the cultivated fruits of the apple, peach, and
cherry trees that grow easily in mountain soil of the region.
An ingenious old hill man, Uncle Op Akers, ferments *sper-
ets* from the pawpaw and persimmon and makes wine from
locust blossoms in addition to using the first two for food.
Descriptions of plant life, both food-producing and otherwise, abound in Stuart's autobiographical book *The Year
of My Rebirth* and in *The Good Spirit* of *Laurel Ridge.*

Stuart shows as intimate a knowledge of the trees of the

region as of the weeds and flowers. All the following trees that Filson noted in Kentucky in 1784 grow on Stuart's seven hundred and fifty acres: several kinds of oak, maple (the *sugar trees* less numerous than in the eighteenth century), honey locust, coffee tree, pappa (pawpaw), cucumber, black mulberry, buckeye (poisonous and hated by cattle owners, as they hated the "poison" laurel), wild cherry. Others recurring in both literal and figurative meanings are hickories, chestnuts (blighted in the 1920s), black walnuts, beeches, butternuts, hazelnuts, poplars (including the tulip tree), sycamores, gums, elms, willows, persimmons, birches, pines, cedars, hemlocks, ash trees, myrtles (in cemeteries), and many others. Kephart's statement that more kinds of trees grow "in thirty miles across the North Carolina mountains than between England and Turkey" probably applies equally well to Stuart's region.

As Stuart looks out over his forests of young timber he can see good basis for his statement that "land in this area will never stay cleared very long after it has been turned back to nature by the people who have tried to conquer it." The sense of identification with nature which makes Stuart feel, as his father and the Hilton men felt, that he is "brother to the tree" has a much more practical basis than poetic fancy. Trees from the coming of the first pioneers sustained the people, giving them food, fuel, furniture, protection, and shelter. Timber cutting and logging have contributed a rugged, earthy strain to hill history and hill character. The perennial *sprouts* in land both cultivated and uncultivated have kept the topsoil from eroding. The woods have sheltered hunters, outlaws, moonshiners, bush-whacking feuders, and repentant sinners at brush arbor revivals, all of whom appear in Stuart's picture of hill life.

Stuart writes of his grandfather Stuart during the presidency of James A. Garfield:

He's cleared more land than any man on the Big Sandy
River. . . . He'd take a lease of thirty acres and get it
clear in the first year. He'd build a log-house on it out'n
the trees he cleared from it, split rails enough from the
oaks and chestnut trees to fence it. He'd get the land to
farm for three years for clearing it, putting a house on it
and fencing it. . . .

He tells how his grandfather snaked out the logs and rafted
them down Sandy and the Ohio to sell them. He gives a detailed account of a house-raising in the short story "Wilburn" and mentions one in *Trees of Heaven*. The frequent
mention of the *chip yard* suggests the source of fuel (although by Stuart's time coal was accessible to many hill
families in the region, which is classified geologically as
part of the Eastern Coalfield). The makeshift activities of
the Tussies in making *house plunder* from the native timber
(and planks from the barn and smokehouse) are a bur-
lesque of the ingenuity of early pioneer adaptation, but
they suggest the possibilities as to what their more energetic
forebears may have achieved in furniture making. Old Op
Akers, though even more the child of nature than the Tussies, said, "I've peeled enough hickory bark in my day to
bottom chairs and use for ropes . . . a body can't get anything to tie with he can trust like hickory bark." Among the
items that show the importance of trees in the everyday
routine of home life and work are log shacks, rail fences,
house plunder, salting troughs, water troughs, *bee-gums,*
well-gums, gambling stick (gambrel), wooden buckets, hoe
and mattock handles, split-bottom chairs and baskets, birdhouses, oakboard coffins (*wooden overcoats*), and bean
poles. All these and more Stuart presents in considerable
detail, most of them in the making as well as in use. Trees,
especially the oak and the hickory, appear on almost every
page of Stuart's writings, sometimes with a touch of homespun humor, but nearly always as symbols of strength and

enduring power, and often showing man's self-indentifica-
tion with the tree. Perhaps because the leaves of the white
oak, stiff and brown, cling to the branches all winter until
new leaves crowd them off in the spring, Stuart uses the
simile of the oak leaf to the point of making it a cliché:
tanned mountain faces and hands are *oak-leaf brown, au-
tumn-leaf-colored,* or *October-leaf-colored* (suggesting sun-
burn). He also reiterates comparisons to *pawpaw leaves bitten by frost* and sassafras leaves. When spring comes, the
old people feel *the sap rising in them;* when old, *their
boughs become sapless.*

The feeling of the hill people for trees, one of many facets of their sense of identification with nature, became involved with sentiment and romance, with superstition and
religion as well as with everyday strength and fortitude.
Subrinea Tussie and Tarvin Bushman bemoaned the *slayin'
of the trees* as they made love under the ailanthus trees, left
standing only because they sheltered the squatters' graves.
Sid Tussie, knowing the family's destitute circumstances,
still "hated to see" the timber cutters "slaughter my *possum-
tailed poplars*" and "my *polecat-tailed pines.*" A timber cutter turned down badly needed wages because he refused to
cut six sugar maples on a hill that sheltered the grave of his
mother. Phoeby in "Plowshare in Heaven" moved a cedar
tree from the other side of Little Sandy so that she would
have something that had grown in the soil of her birthplace.
When the big elm tree on which men had been hanged was
struck by lightning, the hill people found more truth than
humor in the suggestion that "them innocent men they
swung up there . . . got after God Almighty to do something about that tree." When a dead chestnut fell on *weaked*
Anse Bushman, his wife was not surprised that he had
dreams of Hell during his period of unconsciousness that
led him to *get right with God.* When a big oak tree crashed
on Grandma's house during a storm in "The Sanctuary Des-

olated" everyone recognized that she probably preferred such a sudden death dealt by nature to a more long-drawn-out one in a different setting.

Frequently sturdy trees were used as boundary lines for land, written up in the titles and survey reports. In "Testimony of Trees" an old hill man came across Sandy from West Virginia to check the *blazed* scars of the big oak trees along the backbone of the ledge that had been the line for seventy years (the layers of growth from the scars showed the exact year of the survey) and to save his relatives from the land grabbers, who exploited for years the confused state of land titles in Kentucky. Saplings on the place provided Mom with raw materials for making feed baskets during an especially bad winter of illness, cold, and poverty—and the family *made it.* Trees have played a significant part in the history of W-Hollow and the hills above Sandy River.

Stuart the poet loves October, *a beautiful killer,* with yellow leaves tumbling from the poplars, warm-brown leaves rustling from the oaks, orange-red from the dogwoods, red leaves slithering from the sweet gums, persimmons, sumacs; he calls it *October's multi colored death,* and reiterates in dozens of poems the beauty of the autumn hills and the *dead-leaf mood* of autumn sadness.

Almost as pervasive as the flowers, plants, and trees are descriptions of birds, insect, and animal life—and similes deriving from them. The Kentucky hill wild life is inseparable from the setting of forest, hill, and stream.

Although autumn and winter do not kill or drive away all the bird and animal life, the mountain people are much more aware of them in spring and summer. Tarvin and his *squatter gal* Subrinea did not let the loblollies of April mud on their feet or having to chock the wagon wheels to get the wagon around the snake-curved road up the bluff interfere with their enjoyment of the spring flowers they gathered from the nearby banks. Tarvin dated the beginning of spring from the equinoctial thunderstorm:

> ". . . We'll have plenty of wild flowers, green swellin' buds, terrapins, turtles, lizards, frogs and snakes. That's the trumpet that wakes the livin' spring from its long winter sleep."

Stuart the humorist presents a view of awakening animal life as a lovelorn one-eyed hill man saw it. He was too stingy to buy a glass eye unless it would help him to win as his *doughbeater* the beautiful Daisy Locum:

> . . . Redbirds back to the poplar twigs. . . . The sweet smell of green leaves. . . . The woods filled with wild flowers and ferns. Oh, it makes me want a wife more than ever. The birds have wives, the rabbits, the black snakes. . . .

In a similar vein Stuart related the unsuccessful effort of a Methodist hill boy to get a perspective on his "love in the spring" for a hill Baptist girl by realizing that all nature falls in love in the spring. Watching the terrapins, turtles, snakes, and frogs down at the pond only aggravated his disease.

Humor and tragedy are mixed in an unusual story entitled "Dawn of Remembered Spring." The young boy Shan (the name Stuart most often uses in his stories for himself as a boy) avenged the death of his young friend Roy Deer from a water moccasin's bite by clubbing to death with a wild-plum sprout fifty-three snakes in one day. On the way home he thought he saw two copperheads fighting, but his elders smiled and looked at the intertwined bodies with the realization that the deadliest creatures in the hills were making love in the spring. In one of his most sensitive stories, "Another April," Stuart tells from Shan's viewpoint the story of an old man past fourscore years and ten who went out to enjoy April—to talk with his old terrapin friend that lives under the smokehouse in winter and touch the blossoms and budding leaves of the dogwood and redbud trees in the yard, and watch the butterflies. Stuart does not neglect summer, autumn, and winter scenes in his region; but in poem, story, descriptive sketches, and personal history he communicates the beauty, the comedy, the pathos and tragedy of a Kentucky spring.

One of the earliest signs of spring, along with the percoon, and one of the best-loved living things in the Kentucky hills, is the Kentucky cardinal. In the hills the crested male is called the rooster redbird, who along with his mate the henbird, is loved for the beauty of his plumage and his musical calls. Like the bluebird, the robin, and the wren, he will build his nest near people. Songsters also include the meadowlarks, thrushes, pewees (Virginia flycatchers) that kill harmful beetles and flies in the garden, the gray *cornbirds,* and many more. Bright-hued *peckerwoods,* yellow-hammers, *whicker bills,* martins, tiny hummingbirds with wings whirring faster than the eye can see, and various types of sparrows are common. Wild turkeys, pheasant, doves, and whole coveys of wild quail tempt bird hunters. These are only a sampling of the birds in W-Hollow and in Stuart's writings.

The bird lore in Stuart's poems, stories, and autobiographical sketches shows that earth was Stuart's book, as well as his father's and mother's: redbirds sitting on their nests in the rain with dewy drops clinging to their feathers; pheasants wallowing in a sand hole or fearlessly walking across a newly scythed path; quails calling "bobwhite" from the weed fields; gray cornbirds singing in the summer sun; doves (sometimes called *mourning doves*) sounding their plaintive melancholy notes; the whippoorwill nesting on the ground, his evening song signaling time to leave the cornfield for supper, and singing his *lonesome* night calls; *rain crows* croaking for rain in dry weather; *shike-pokes* flying; noisy *peckerwoods* drilling in dead trees; martins hurrying to their boxes just before a storm breaks; starlings robbing the cornfield; V-shaped flocks of wild geese flying South just before cold weather; chicken hawks and screech owls preying upon the chickens; buzzards floating in lazy circles waiting for something to die; the scream of the nighthawk and the *who-whooo* of the owls. These night birds evoke feelings of loneliness in people living almost literally *so far back that the hoot owls holler in the daytime.* These are a few of the innumerable details of bird life that Stuart has written from observation and memory, much of the lore passed down to him by his father and mother.

> I have often thought that in the wild life of the high hills everything was waiting for something to die to eat its flesh. The wild dogs killed the sheep and cows, the buzzards and the crows sailed above and waited for their share of them. The foxes killed the birds, rabbits, and chickens. The hound dogs killed the foxes. All forms of life preyed on the rabbit—even the snake.

"Life preys upon life here," mused Tarvin Bushman as he watched a flock of crows discover a dead sheep and feed upon it in the snow, two of their number meanwhile keeping guard and caw-cawing in the trees above. While the *yowes* (ewes) were lambing, Tarvin killed almost three hundred crows, enough to made a big *doodle* of black feathers beside the sheep shanty. On a hot summer day mountain men watch the buzzards circling overhead and think, "Sign of dead stock, signs of death."

A natural association explains a superstitious mountain man's embodiment of death in the form of a turkey buzzard; humor prevailed when the one-eyed mountain man found himself competing unsuccessfully for his sweetheart's affections with the unseasonable call of a whippoorwill in daytime and in the fall; more pathos than humor emerges from "Eyes of an Eagle," the story of an aged ex-sharpshooter who could no longer hit the dirty, grain-eating starlings nesting near his house; Stuart assigns to fact the story of a mountain man's setting fire to a chicken-stealing owl, which then flew into the elements—seemingly immune to gunshots—destroying fields, timber tracts, barns, fences, and two houses so that it took several *workin's* to pacify the neighbors.

Insect lore, factual and traditional in Stuart, provides a good deal of straight-faced humor on the part of such characters as Uncle Op as well as a good deal of scientific detail from the viewpoint of the observant layman—more often in individualized imagery than in lists such as the following one. Butterflies, jar flies (cicadas), tobacco-spitting grasshoppers, June bugs, doodlebugs, katydids, crickets, ants, mud daubers, snake feeders, sweat bees, hornets, wasps, honeybees, boring bumblebees, and spiders are part of a mountain summer.

Op, who never missed an opportunity to enjoy himself at the expense of the city-bred Alf, recited an elaborate scheme for telling the time of day and night by the insects, birds, and animals, burlesquing a true-to-life habit the hill man developed of telling time quite haphazardly by nature's signs rather than by clock watching—measuring time, as Alf expressed it, "by what President was in office and by the nesting seasons of the birds." Alf preferred not to measure time by bee stings, nor did he accept sweat bee stings as God's way of speeding up a lazy man in the cornfield; he preferred his electric clock to timing himself by early-morning snails and doodlebugs and at night by stars, katydids, nightjars, and foxes.

Of more practical benefit to old Op and many other mountain people in the old days was the honeybee. Few mountain homes were without a row of bee-gums, such as Stuart describes in "Saving the Bees" and "Big Drone and Little Drone." He gives them more casual mention elsewhere. Op used wild honey instead of the sugar it would have cost money to buy or the sorghum it would have been more trouble to make. *Coursing bees* to bee trees (and they do make a beeline with unerring sense of direction) and then robbing the bees when the honey is in the combs satisfied some people like Old Op; but most families cut the section of the bee tree (not always a gum tree) and moved it near the house (some found it easier to capture the bees and hive them in boxes): "It [the beehive] was just a cut from the sourwood tree we'd sawed down and Pa nailed planks over the end."

Other types of bees less desirable are the boring bumble-bees, which Stuart found making holes in the eaves of his house (not all bumblebees are of this type); yellow jackets (Stuart solved a problem by depositing frogs near a nest of them); hornets, which build long, hanging nests "as large as a three-gallon lard bucket and shaped like a pear, with the little end hanging downward," do not sting unless molested, but then are "harder to handle than a polecat under the bed or a bear in the kitchen."

For the most part, spiders are more involved with the hill man's folklore than with imperiling his life, but in several stories Stuart mentions the poisonous bite of a certain variety of spider. Stuart makes comedy of an almost fatal spider bite in the story of a moonshine addict who has *spiders* (or *snakes*) *in his boots;* the horse-quart of hot moonshine simultaneously cures the poison, kills the victim's taste for whisky, and wins the woman he has *sparked* for fourteen years. As a matter of fact, both the poisonous black widow and the fiddler spiders are fairly common in Kentucky.

Anthills in Stuart's yard at W-Hollow gave him an opportunity to observe at close range (during the summer of his convalescence from his heart attack) a battle to the death of both armies between black and red ants. During that summer he was much aware of the cicada, or *jarfly* with his churring monotonous song; of the grasshoppers, the June bugs, fireflies (*lightning bugs*), crickets, katydids, gnats, and bees. In short stories and novels he mentions the four-winged *snake feeders* showing where the snakes were in the waters below until the birds swooped from the willows along the bank and snatched them, the mud daubers' and wasps' nests in the abandoned house Grandpa Tussie moved into after the eviction from the big Rayburn house not long before his death. In the following Stuart has adapted the symbolism of the spider and the fly: (of dying Grandpa Tussie) *Time had been the spider that had sapped the life from Grandpa;* Mammon was the spider that lured men to leave their fields and permit themselves to be exploited for the gain of people beyond the hills; *a durned big stripped-tail spider* is a death symbol to the man having nightmare deliriums following a mine accident.

Stuart does not forget to sing the poetic beauty of a firefly ballet on a July night with the crickets, the cicadas, the bass of the frogs, and the far-off solo notes of the whippoorwill as an orchestra; or pathos in the picture of simple-minded Run-around Jack coming home from the range to chase butter-flies all day on Laurel Ridge on a summer day; grotesque humor in the battle of the bee-gum thief, who must battle his own bees; squalor in the scene of the houseflies swarm-ing on the unwashed dishes in the kitchen of the squatter Tussies' open-doored shack. Stuart reflects a real signifi-cance of insects in the life of the hills.

If birds and insects abound in Stuart's writings, reptiles are ubiquitous. The poisonous copperhead which strikes without warning has brought tragedy into many mountain families, as the thinly fictionized real-life occurrences in Stuart's stories show. The rattlesnake and the water moccasin are the only other reptiles in W-Hollow that bite with deadly venom; but black snakes (egg thieves, but insect killers), cow snakes, house snakes, other harmless varieties, and lizards (sometimes incorrectly called scorpions) appear in essays, poems, and stories. In *Album of Destiny* bull black snake, copperhead, gray lizard, green scorpion, and other reptiles—along with the whispering grass, the autumn wind, the voice of spring, and human voices of both living and dead—speak poems of the mountain setting and mountain life.

"Snakes—snakes," Mom used to say, "are goin' to run us out'n this Hollow." She, Grandpa Birdwell, and Old Op survived copperhead bites; some of Brother Fain Groan's followers survived the bites of *grave copperheads* when they tried to resurrect Sister Groan, and some did not. Roy Deer died of a water moccasin bite. Presented as factual, not as tall tale, is Mom's killing a six-foot-long house snake with a bed slat and killing two cow snakes resting on the wall plate with a goose-neck hoe; and Pa's killing twenty-eight copperheads in a two-acre oat field above the house during one spring season. Tall tales and superstitions as well as folk and Stuart similes are reminders of the hill man and hill woman's continual awareness of snakes. A vivid metaphor shows the tenacity of the copperhead, which will not run from danger—after fire has run through W-Hollow, he is *a white whiplash of ashes.*

Dogs are sometimes trained and some learn in self-defense to kill copperheads. A notable illustration is Stuart's own dog Black Boy, which he fictionizes in the book *Mongrel Mettle* (from the dog's point of view) and in several short stories.

It may be true that snakes do not bite unless frightened or angered; but many mountain men, women, and children have been bitten unawares.

In *Album of Destiny* a moralizing poem, attributed to

Bull Blacksnake, presents an interesting facet of Stuart's identification of man with the wild creatures:

> Why do you call your fellow man a "snake"
> When he has wronged you in some sort of way
> And nearly caused your human heart to break?
>
> We better snakes war Copperhead's vile clan,
> Our rattling tails drum music when we fight!
> We snakes go through our lives each with one lover.
>
> Few men attain the honor of "a snake."

Old Op expressed the idea in relation to water moccasins and turtles: "wild things in nature get along better'n most human folks." Especially since his heart attack, Stuart has noted repeatedly the miracle of hibernation for the cold-blooded animals of the earth, and the renewing power of rest.

Lizards are acclaimed the best of flycatchers, as they slither through the grass and over rocks; scorpions cling to the bark of trees (these little gray creatures are a type of lizard, not poisonous scorpions); mud turtles live in the mud of mountain pools (some people have a taste for the meat and soup made from them); terrapins that live a century or more feed in the gardens of tolerant hill farmers; frogs make themselves heard in every swamp and hollow; toads eat mosquitoes, gnats, moths, horseflies, and other insects annoying to man.

Stuart's frequent mention of these creatures is in keeping with the hill farmer's friendly feeling for them. He uses folk similes and adaptations of folk similes as well as original coinages in making figurative use of these cold-blooded creatures of the Hollow. Favorite similes in this category are that a man's *Adam's apple ran up and down like a tree frog,* and he *laughs like a big-throated bullfrog.*

Fish receive passing mention in many passages, but play a negligible part in the life of Stuart's region as compared with the game animals. Op caught *suckers,* bass and *red hoss;* Billy Auxier fished for *mudcats* with red worms (earthworms), cutworms, grubworms, and locusts; a hill-man illegally netted carp and catfish near Tygart River dam; Stuart mentions that *crawdads* are not good bait, and refers to pin-hooking minnows and using them for bait. The cray-fish cut the corn roots in the *crawdad bottoms* down along the creek one year and ruined the crop, bringing on the *dark winter* that Stuart has written of in "Spring Victory" and "Dark Winter" as well as in *Beyond Dark Hills.* Stuart sometimes uses *crawdad* in the figurative sense of trying to withdraw from a situation or a bargain, even *crawdaded backwards* of the attitude of a girl toward an amorous swain. In Stuart's time fishing seems to have been more for plea-sure than for food.

Denning in hollow trees, under rock cliffs, burrowing in the earth, and crawling, climbing, slinking, scurrying every-where in the forest are small animals. Bears, deer, wildcats, panthers, wolves are seldom seen; but rabbits, ground squir-rels, gray squirrels, opossums, raccoons, groundhogs, wea-sels, skunks (polecats), foxes are still numerous (though less so than a generation ago). Stuart knows and writes of their usefulness to the hill people, and of their habitats and their destructiveness, of the pleasure and inconvenience they have caused.

The mountain people are almost unanimous in liking the meat of the gray squirrel and the rabbit; and many of them eat, or have eaten, possum, coon, and groundhog. "When a man gits so he can't eat squirrel broth he is liable to *kick the bucket,*" is the opinion of many mountain people. Espe-cially with regard to rabbits, Stuart reflects that rapid mul-tiplying of these small hunted animals keeps a balance of nature. "Weasels ain't no good," says a mountain woman in *Hie to the Hunters;* "all they're fit fer is to cut the throats of chickens and rabbits and drink their blood. Hides ain't worth much." Moles, too, do more harm than good, most farmers think. The minks, skunks, possums, foxes, coons are no longer abundant enough to contribute more than pin money for schoolboys in most sections of the hills; but the sport of hunting them is a significant part of mountain life, and animal lore is significent in folk beliefs.

The total resources of the environment, utilized by primitive methods which only education and better roads could change, yielded at best a poor living as judged by the standards of twentieth-century urban America. Stuart is typical of his people in that he has never let the hardships and hazards of a mountain winter or the backbreaking toil of *making the crop* in the *smothery* heat of summer blind him to the fresh beauty of a mountain April or the October splendor of hills aflame with autumn color. But he has also recognized that those young men and women who went beyond their hills to attend school, to work in industrial plants, or to participate in World War II could not return to the old way of life: ". . . How can we remain isolated when our youth have fought all over the world, when they are practically all finished high school, and a solid minority of them are going to college?" Stuart sees this loss of isolation, however, as a mixed blessing; for "winter isolation used to give us time to rebuild our individual selves." He sympathizes with those who think they would like to return to the old way of life, but he cannot forget the hardships and the physical labor that made up that life.

No one else in Stuart's community has equaled his contribution toward making the outside world aware of the beauty of the hill setting or of making known the needs of his people for economic stability. "The longest pole will reach the highest persimmons" was written in another context; but it applies to the native son who has lectured and written vividly and vigorously to promote a better way of life for his people. Not only his articles on education, but also the "casual yet familiar way of life" set forth in his stories has implied a social protest even when the main focus has been on humor, nostalgia for tradition, romantic appreciation of the hill setting, or personal tragedy.

A present-day visitor to W-Hollow, returning after an absence of twenty or thirty years, would at first be impressed with how little the landscape has changed: the same lush summer growth in the uncultivated creek bottoms, the same timbered hills, grassy pastures with the incorrigible sprouts growing here and there, the corn and tobacco fields; the same bony ridges of hills outlined against the gray sky of winter; the same beauty of spring and autumn. The first difference he would note would almost surely be that hardly a place in the community is inaccessible to him by car—although the graveled and surfaced roads might take him across many small bridges and might be more narrow than in more heavily traveled areas of the state.

Then he would notice that most of the houses have been weatherboarded, and that telephone and electric wires lead into most of them. He would notice the scattering of television aerials, and at almost every farm a car, a truck, or both parked in the lane or near the barn. In the fields he would see a tractor instead of a span of mules pulling the plow, or a combine instead of cradle and scythe cutting grain at harvest time. He would notice the pump house built over the old well and the running water faucets in the kitchen.

In the houses he would see chenille bedspreads and blankets on the old-fashioned cord beds in the same households with the homemade quilts and coverlets of an earlier day; upholstered furniture in the living room, and the old hickory split-bottom chairs on the porch or in the yard; perhaps an electric mixer in the kitchen where once the old coffee mill stood, an electric washer instead of the outdoor iron kettle and galvanized tub. He would notice bric-a-brac, utensils, and supplies in the most old-fashioned homes that show the influence of the modern shops and supermarkets.

Men's clothing, still comfortably casual and unpretentious, and the women's cotton house dresses would still look old-fashioned in contrast with the young city couples' shorts and shirts; but certainly not now *Elizabethan*. He would see few bearded men; and many of the women would have permanent waves in their hair.

As for food, the hill family still takes pride in the quality and quantity of home-grown fruits and vegetables it can produce, and many of them still raise their own meats, prizing Kentucky country ham above all others; but the deep-freeze storage unit is not uncommon as a replacement for the old cellar and smokehouse. The hill woman is not likely to take kindly to the pressure cooker, and she will still use more grease and longer cooking time for preparing meats and vegetables than her lowland contemporaries; but she may have an electric cookstove.

Stuart in recent writings has made clear that the isolation of the past has left the hills, and that only here and there in the language and in the customs do some vestiges survive from the older culture of his youth.

Here this books ends its tour of Jesse Stuart's Kentucky. For those readers who know Stuart's work, it has been a tour through familiar country. They recognize here his most frequently stressed themes. For those readers to whom this book is an introduction, *Beyond Dark Hills, Trees of Heaven,* and *Taps for Private Tussie* will lead to an intimate acquaintance with those aspects of Appalachia treated here. Those who wish to range further into Stuart's by-paths may choose among more than thirty other book titles and hundreds of periodical publications of poems, articles, and stories.

An Appreciation

Jesse Stuart has the strength to follow his own bent as a writer. He has not tried to be *avant-garde,* obscure, nihilist, precious, nor has he used any other transparent literary device to appear wiser than he is. Testimony to his common touch is seen in the warm responses he has elicited from people of other races and nationalities in all walks of life during his travels and teaching abroad.

He could have used his successes as an author to buy comfortable exile in a sunny climate or a city penthouse. Other American authors have done it, but theirs was a different kind of dedication—often to anger and rejection. Stuart's sense of identity with his Kentucky, the key to his success, has directed his efforts toward preservation of the good and the beautiful by letting others see them through his eyes.

He has not withdrawn into hand wringing or futile protest over the manifold problems of Appalachian transition. He has, rather, exposed personal and social backwardness by hyperbolic comedy. Even when dealing with the least desirable traits of his culture he can be uproariously funny, driving out evil with laughter instead of tears.

Although comedy is one of his most effective devices, he knows when to be sober, when to turn to "serious truthful talk." The tender emotions of young love and courtship, as in *Daughter of the Legend,* can tug at the heart strings of any reader whose outlook on life has not been corrupted by false values. He accentuates the positive.

The wonder of Nature's eternal cycle of birth, death, and resurrection underlies his entire range of writing. Seeing "into the life of things" in W-Hollow has given Stuart a voice to speak of the universal human experience. Metaphors and symbols are almost surely best when they are least private and arbitrary. *Trees of Heaven* is such a natural metaphor for Stuart's theme. The earth, the snakes and lizards, the whispering wind and grass, the changing seasons are inevitable symbols in the poems of *Album of Destiny. Year of My Rebirth* is the view from Stuart's window in W-Hollow, a wider view than most of us ever see, expressing his love of earth and sky and all living things. It is a world seething and bursting with life and meaning.

To see the universe in a grain of sand or a leaf of grass— to state or imply a universal truth in terms of a particular —these are the abilities of a great writer and qualities of great literature of all time. Jesse Stuart is a regional writer, yes, but his region transcends geographical boundaries. Jesse Stuart's Kentucky, so rich in authentic detail—from highly localized peculiarities of speech to such a rare Elizabethan hangover as frog-trouncing—becomes a token of the world at large. And Stuart the author, by cultivating faithfully his knowledge and understanding of his microcosm, has emerged as a citizen of the world, a man of all seasons, a specialist and a universalist.

Humanity is never abstract or general to Stuart, but he has known enough of the Fronnies and Sals, the Micks, Jeffs, and Ops, the Shans, Finns and Tarvins, the Johns and Kathaleens to trust the future. Contemporary literature has need of his buoyant certainties.

A Bibliographical Commentary

When I first set out to do a study of Jesse Stuart's work, it was prompted by the recognition that his family and environment were similar to my own in many respects. I knew from firsthand experience that his material was authentic. The study began in 1953 and ended its first phase as a doctoral dissertation, "Folklore of the Cumberlands as Reflected in the Writings of Jesse Stuart," at the University of Pennsylvania in 1960. But a dissertation, especially one with introduction, bibliography, appendices, and no fewer than 1,330 footnotes is hardly a readable book! It is too clogged with "scholarly" apparatus to let the information flow through.

This book was undertaken with a resolution to avoid cluttering its pages with even so much as a single footnote. I have kept that resolution, but it seems proper to include here at the end a few notes for those readers curious enough to seek additional information about Jesse Stuart and his Kentucky.

CHAPTER ONE

Stuart's folk songs are regional variants of traditional songs that have been collected and studied by many authorities. The texts of songs included here have been compared with those found in *The Ballad Book* by MacEdward Leach (Harper, 1955) and *The Folk Songs of North America in the English Language* by Alan Lomax (Doubleday, 1960). More specific information on some texts appears in *Traditional Ballads of Virginia* by A. K. Davis, Jr. (Harvard University Press, 1929), The Frank C. Brown Collection of *North Carolina Folklore* (Duke University Press, 1952–1964), and Cecil Sharp's *English Folk Songs from the Southern Appalachians* (ed. by Maude Karpeles, 2 vols. London: Oxford University Press, 1932).

North Carolina Folklore is also a very useful reference for checking out medicinal uses of plants, beliefs, and superstitions. For the latter, one should also consult an earlier work, *Kentucky Superstitions* by D. L. and L. B. Thomas (Princeton University Press, 1920). For both folk beliefs and traditional elements of narratives, one should consult the *Motif-Index of Folk Literature* by Stith Thompson (Indiana University Press, 1955–1957). Stuart uses much real history and still more legend, or pseudo-history. For these, read *A History of Kentucky* by Thomas D. Clark (Prentice-Hall, 1937). See other works by the same author for authentic details on many other aspects of Kentucky. A significant number of all these folkloristic elements have also appeared in the *Kentucky Folklore Record* (quarterly publication of the Kentucky Folklore Society, Western Kentucky University, 1955 ff.).

CHAPTER TWO

Some of the more extreme forms of fundamental doctrine as preached and practiced by illiterate or semiliterate hill preachers and their congregations incorporate many aspects of folklore mentioned above. Some comic distortions or misinterpretations of Scripture are, of course, traditional enough to be classed as traveling anecdotes. I personally observed some of the serio-comic events associated with the bright display of the aurora borealis Stuart has depicted in *Foretaste of Glory.* The glory-bound repentant sinners turned up at school the next morning looking rather sheepish. Consult *Religions in the Development of American Culture* by William W. Sweet (Scribner's, 1952) for more information about the proliferation of sects. "The Folk-Life of a Kentucky Mountain Community," a master's thesis written by Marie Campbell (George Peabody College, 1937), provides additional information concerning visions and their significance to older mountain women.

The folk song aspects of traditional gospel tunes are greatly clarified in *White Spirituals in the Southern Uplands* by George Pullen Jackson (University of North Carolina Press, 1933). Thomas D. Clark discusses the practical religious beliefs of the Kentucky mountain community in his *A History of Kentucky.*

My own field informants have given me many accounts of foot washing and outdoor baptism. These practices are current, and may be observed quite conveniently. For additional discussion of laying a corpse and settin'-up, see *Ozark Superstitions* by Vance Randolph (Columbia University Press, 1947).

The talent for "lining out" a song and "rolling" the notes of the songs in the *Old Sweet Songster* is current also. I have a tape recording of an excellent performance of this kind made within a few weeks of this writing: the performer lives in Paintsville, Kentucky.

CHAPTER THREE

The frolics in the hills as reflected in Stuart's writing and elsewhere contain elements so frequently recorded that they are probably the best-known aspects of Kentucky folk life. Play parties, square dances, and singing schools have received so much attention, especially during recent years of the urban "folk" revival, that a stereotype of the banjo-picking, dance-calling Kentuckian has emerged. Jean Ritchie's *Singing Family of the Cumberlands* (Oxford University Press, 1955) does much to add to our knowledge of these forms of homemade entertainment.

Although I found no allusions to a Frog-Trouncing Day outside of Stuart's pages, one of my informants in Wayne County, West Virginia, described this cruel sport with details closely paralleling those Stuart presented.

The deplorable carnival atmosphere at public hangings and the "last good night" of the doomed victim are a matter of public record. See, for example, the description of a hanging in "In Search of a Ballad," by O. J. Wilson, *Kentucky Folklore Record*, January–March, 1967.

For a wealth of detail on feuding, moonshining, lawing, and other aspects of the code of the hills, see *The Southern Highlander and His Homeland* by John C. Campbell (1931); see also *Big Sandy Valley* by Willard Rouse Jillson (1923) and other publications by the same author; see also *Land of the Saddlebags* by James Watt Raine (1924).

CHAPTER FOUR

The Thread That Runs So True is autobiographical, but it is more; it comes closest to "protest" in Stuart's works. Joy Elmer Morgan, editor of the *National Education Association Journal*, reviewed the book enthusiastically (January, 1950), expressing the opinion that it was good history, good literature, and good pedagogy, a book that all American teachers should read.

According to Stuart, this book is also widely used in relation to teacher education in several countries of Africa and the Near East.

Inadequate facilities have long been a scandal in public education. Thomas D. Clark, in his *A History of Kentucky* (p. 509), wrote: "In 1887 the commissioner from Woodford County said he was faced with the embarrassing situation of getting his people to understand that a Woodford County child is worth as much as a race horse, and is entitled to as good a house in which to study." Concerning outmoded books, Clark cited the experience of a county superintendent who said (p. 511) he "virtually had to call out the state militia to get rid of Webster's *Blue Back Spelling Book.*"

Kentucky Public School Statistics (Bureau of Administration and Finance, Frankfort, June, 1966) gives a table showing a ten-year trend of diminishing numbers of small schools. There were, for example, 1,801 one-teacher schools in Kentucky for the school year of 1956–1957; there were 422 in 1965–1966. A five-year table for the average salaries for Kentucky schoolteachers showed $3,412 in 1959–1960, increased to $5,192 in 1965–1966. The increase is substantial, but the lag is still present in terms of what teachers receive in many other states.

Stuart's battle against outmoded trustee administration

has been won. *Kentucky School Statistics* reports that the state had in June, 1966, 120 county districts and 80 independent districts, a total of 200 basic administrative units.

CHAPTER FIVE

Stuart's many allusions to work make it quite clear that he has a sense of nostalgic love for work associated with farming, and resigned acceptance of work associated with industry. He draws from personal experience for his description of either kind, and he draws from the memories of his elders for activities that had become outmoded before his time.

Clark (*A History of Kentucky*) relates the background of political rivalry involved in the tobacco war and the reign of the night riders; the legislation removing the tax from mountaineers' dogs; and the tobacco panic of 1921.

The Plight of the Bituminous Coal Miner by Homer Lawrence Morris (University of Pennsylvania Press, 1934) gives a detailed account of the boom of the industry from 1890 to 1927 and retrenchment (beginning in 1928 and accelerated by the stock-market crash of 1929) which brought about complete disorganization.

For a mountain farmer's attitude toward work in the coal mine (after the crops are *laid by*) see Stuart's "Vacation in Hell," *Esquire*, July, 1938.

Indicative of the glacial slowness of needed reform when powerful interests wish to impede it is the long delay in legislating reasonable controls for strip mining in Kentucky. Although the urgent need for this type of conservation has been apparent for decades, effective control measures were not enacted into law until 1966, and even then it was against bitter opposition.

CHAPTER SIX

Jesse Stuart's home in W-Hollow, like his Kentucky, is a blend of the old and the new. Prominently located near the front of the house is a well, complete with *well sweep* and bucket, although there is running water in the house. The smokehouse is hidden from sight at the back, and it has been converted from a structure for preserving meat to a separate study for the author. Everywhere, inside and out, are reminders of an older, more rigorous way of life, but they are reminders only, for Stuart, like his neighbors, has accepted the inevitable tide of "progress" in rural areas. Yet the reminders in Stuart country are fresh and numerous enough to make one aware of lingering pioneer traits—in speech, in mores, in an independence of spirit not always backed up by independence of means.

For another view of a similar situation, read Vance Randolph's *The Ozarks: An American Survival of Primitive Society* (Vanguard, 1931). See also Howard Washington Odum's *The Way of the South* (Macmillan, 1947).

For an up-to-date commentary on the plight of Appalachia, read Harry M. Caudill's *Night Comes to the Cumberlands* (Little, 1963) and Jack E. Weller's *Yesterday's People: Life in Contemporary Appalachia* (University of Kentucky Press, 1965). For a reporter's probing with camera and questions, see John Fetterman's *Stinking Creek* (Dutton, 1967). A quarterly periodical emanating from the area and well worth an interested reader's time is *Mountain Life & Work*, published at Berea, Kentucky, by the Council of the Southern Mountains.

Books by Jesse Stuart

1954 A Penny's Worth of Character
1955 Red Mule
1956 The Year of My Rebirth
1958 Plowshare in Heaven
1960 The Rightful Owner
1960 God's Oddling
1960 Huey the Engineer
1961 Andy Finds a Way
1962 Hold April
1963 A Jesse Stuart Reader
1964 Save Every Lamb
1965 A Jesse Stuart Harvest
1965 Daughter of the Legend
1966 My Land Has a Voice
1966 A Ride with Huey the Engineer
1967 Mr. Gallion's School

1965 Short Stories for Discussion,
edited by Albert K. Rideout and Jesse Stuart

Translations (various works) into German, Swedish, Norwegian, Danish, Portuguese, Spanish, French, Italian, Polish, Czech, Russian, Arabic, Bengali, Telegu, Urdu, Taiwanese.

[Adapted from Hensley C. Woodbridge, *Jesse Stuart: A Bibliography,* Lincoln Memorial University Press, 1960; and "Jesse Stuart: A Bibliography for May, 1960–May, 1965," *The Register of the Kentucky Historical Society,* Vol. 63, No. 4 (October, 1965), pp. 349–370.]

Index

About the Author

MARY WASHINGTON CLARKE, like Jesse Stuart, was born and brought up in the hills of Appalachia. She has taught journalism and creative writing at the high school level, American literature and folklore at several state universities, and is now Professor of English at Western Kentucky University. Her two previous books are *Introducing Folklore* and *A Folklore Reader,* both co-authored by her husband.